EMPOWERED TO BE FREE

William T. Bantom III

MANIFOLD GRACE
Publishing House LLC

Empowered to Be Free
Copyright © 2014 William T. Bantom III

Cover design: Kingdom Marketing Solutions Inc.

All Scripture is King James Version unless otherwise noted. See references for complete list

ISBN: 978-1-937400-42-2
ISBN: 978-1-937400-43-9 ebook

Printed in the United States of America

Revised April, 2015

Manifold Grace Publishing House, LLC
Southfield, Michigan 48033
www.manifoldgracepublishinghouse.com

Dedication

To the loving memory of my mother
Beatrice M. Bantom,
January 29, 1922 – June 15, 2014

Acknowledgments

A word of gratitude is due to many who have impacted my life in positive ways throughout the years. It is of the utmost importance that I openly thank a few of them at this time.

Let me start with my wife Loretta, the love of my life and greatest gift God has given me next to salvation. I can't thank you enough or fully capture in words what your love, prayer, support, and encouragement has meant to my life. I truly would not be the man I am today without you.

Next I want to thank my publisher, Darlene Dickson, at Manifold Grace Publishing House for her guidance and unwavering support throughout this project.

Lastly I want to thank my pastor and spiritual father, Bishop Ben Gibert, for revelation, impartation and being the Hebrew 6:12 model for me to follow and pattern my life after.

Contents

Foreword

"Empowered to Be Free" is a revelation walk out of your personal prisons to a powerfully free life in Christ. Minister William Bantom carefully prescribes dynamic, Biblical principles to help you realize what bondage makes you do, to motivate you in what Christ frees you to consistently be. This book is a roadmap. Every chapter teaches you powerful steps, keys and principles on how to leave addictions, bondage and reciprocal failure, life patterns, and then travel forward with handles to choose, be sustained by and empowered to live personally and spiritually free through Jesus Christ (John 8: 31-36).

I have watched Minister Bantom painstakingly and passionately explain these principles with men and women in every setting possible. We have watched, cried - believed with Will and his wife Loretta—to see Will pour out these principles from the streets of the worst parts of Detroit to men's classes in churches, to gymnasiums, to conventions, to large crowds resulting in many, many, many changed, saved, transformed, delivered and freed lives. We have seen him pour over and pray through the principles outlined in these pages many times from very early in the morning to very late at night to hone what God would say through what the principles ask you to do.

As a former Co-Director of a Teen Challenge intake center for drug addicts in California (Doxa House), current Elder of Detroit World Outreach and CEO of Bridge Networks, I have seen Minister Bantom keep pressing for the best-life transformation ways possible to explain how you can walk in the highest level of freedom for your life and those you affect. I and my wife, Shari (Author of *Walking in Wholeness*—Freedom from Molestation and Abuse-Trauma to Triumph) completely endorse Minister William Bantom and this epic discipleship book.

I wish we had this book 40+ years ago during and in the aftermath of the Jesus movement. So many of us with substance abuse experimentation or addiction problems (hundreds of thousands) met Jesus, made bad choices, felt condemned, bound, and then went back to the cesspool of the world. Many of us lost "it" (A Freed life in Christ), because we just didn't have a valued resource like *Empowered to Be Free* to guide us. Today, we need this now more than ever. We need to; we must - in this generation, for our children and our children's children -- use it or lose "it".

You will literally be blown away by the key principle studies, ponder points, chapter reflections and meditations, case studies and personal testimonies all aimed at helping you make choices to get free and stay free. This book is hard core, road tested and usable in settings from the suburban classroom to the urban recreation center. Everyone—seriously-- from the experienced teacher to the first time student; will really get into and be changed by what they find on every page of *"Empowered to Be Free"*.

Pastors Arthur and Shari Ledlie
January 4, 2015

Introduction

Addictions, bondage and patterns of poor decision making that seem to keep your life stagnant, are not topics most people want to openly tackle. We hide them in the dark recesses of our minds, not wanting the light to shine on our failures, mistakes and weaknesses. We hope we will wake up one day and things will automatically have changed for the better, our past mistakes will be covered up and the cycle of repeated defeat will be forever broken. We know, on the inside, this is probably an unrealistic expectation but since it's all we have to hold onto, letting it go would be to give up all hope for a better life. So, we just hold on day after day, year after year, becoming more emotionally drained and more spiritually defeated.

For the record this is not a condition that I read about, this was my actual day-to-day dilemma for many years of my life. I was a Christian, I knew God, had a personal relationship with God and had logged hundreds of hours in corporate and personal Bible study, yet there was no consistent evidence of the promises of God *NO FRUIT* working for me. During this time in my life I tried everything I could think of to get free. I got baptized three or four times, got hands laid on me and made multiple trips to rehab. I even went to a deliverance service where I was told I could get rid of the demons by vomiting them into a paper bag. For the record, nothing I tried worked. This helped the enemy convince me I was so messed up that God no longer loved me, therefore the promises in His Word were not meant for me. At this point I actually believed the lies of the enemy, lost all hope and even attempted suicide.

Thanks be to God He didn't just save me from death. He rescued me from my sin, restored my faith in Him, and showed me in His Word how to live free from the bondage, addictions and the poor decision making patterns that kept me from living the abundant life God sent Christ to make available. My prayer for this writing is to spare you from going through what I went through to get free and stay free. The Bible tells us in Hebrews 6:12 that we are to follow those who, through faith and patience, inherit God's promises. This doesn't negate experience as a good teacher but it does negate the fact that is has to be your own personal experience that you learn from.

Around my seventeenth year of freedom from various addictions and unproductive patterns of thinking and behaving, while helping to facilitate an addiction recovery program at my church, I sensed the Lord telling me to get a Bible based program to help others experience the freedom I now enjoyed. I remember going home to tell my wife who immediately told me the Lord wasn't telling me to find a program; He was commissioning me to write one. After months of praying and fasting we launched Empowered to Be Free, a thirty-two week program that has since changed the lives of many. I believe the seven key principles taught in this book will help you to fortify your faith in God, guide you in some critical areas of pursuing God and help you take on the mind and manner of Christ. Additionally it will reveal truths that will transform you and empower you to be free, live free and maximize the threefold intent of the gift of freedom in your life.

It should also be understood that this book is not written from the perspective of a theologian or biblical scholar nor is it meant to be an exhaustive study of the topics covered within. It's simply a practical application of seven key biblical principles that changed my life and empowered many others to live free. There is no quick fix or magic potion because true and lasting change requires hard work and consistency. I have learned that the promises of God are triggered by the principles of God which are lived on a day to day basis through consistent practical application.

May God bless you on your journey to living a life beyond your dreams.

Chapter One:

Freedom and Empowerment

So Jesus said to those Jews who had believed in Him, If you abide in My word [hold fast to My teachings and live in accordance with them], you are truly My disciples. ³² And you will know the Truth, and the Truth will set you free. John 8:31-32 (AMP)

If you were to be brutally honest you would have to admit that most believers live a life plagued with bondages and perpetual frustrations because biblical promises are not being realized in their lives. It is not because they're bad people who don't love God, and don't want to please God. It's because they are stuck and don't know how to get free. Many have tried all kinds of programs that guarantee a quick fix, but I'm sorry to tell you - there is no quick fix for bondage and stagnation. It is a mindset that takes *Diligence* time, intentional effort, revelation from God and commitment to overcome. It is not a one step process, but a commitment to a lifestyle of learning to live and have faith in the Word and power of God.

John 8:36 says *"Therefore if the Son shall make you free, you shall be free indeed"* (MKJV). This is a powerful statement with a very important promise that warrants having a basic understanding of what it actually means. Let's look at three key observations from that verse. First, Jesus Christ, not we ourselves, is the one who sets us free. Secondly, the words "make free" means "to liberate from the bondage of sin, deliver or cause to be unrestricted". Thirdly, the word 'indeed' means "truly, in reality and as a matter of fact". In summary, this verse means, it is a true

- 1 -

and unchangeable fact that anyone who has accepted Jesus as Lord and Savior has been made free from the bondage of sin and death. They have been given the authority to make unrestricted decisions and therefore have the authority to determine for themselves the course of their life.

Now, if you are not a believer, and have not accepted Jesus as Lord, John 8:36 does not apply to you. In Ephesians 2, the Bible actually describes the unbeliever as being in the world without God, disconnected from the promises of God and therefore left without hope. This person is left without the ability or authority to resist the lust of their flesh, the lure of the world or the devil's attempts to destroy their lives. If this is you and you don't have a personal relationship with God, I pray that you ask yourself right now if you want to continue the course that you are on or do you want to be empowered to be free to live the abundant life that only Christ can make available. The choice is simply that you believe Jesus Christ is the son of God who died for your sins. If your choice is Christ, Romans 10:9-10 tells us if you confess the Lord Jesus with your mouth and believe in your heart that God raised Him from the dead, you shall be saved. This simply means if you have a heartfelt conviction that Jesus is alive and you are willing to receive Him as your Lord and Savior you are ready to pray a prayer that will lead you into salvation. All you have to do at this point is say the following prayer aloud and you will be saved:

Then you must live like a believer

> "Lord God I thank you for your son Jesus, who came, died and rose again just for me. I thank you that His blood washes me and cleanses me from all sin, guilt and shame. I receive Jesus now as my Lord and savior. I ask that you would mold me and shape me into the person you created me to be and guide me into a life that accomplishes your purpose and leads me to the good life that brings true fulfillment through you. In Jesus name I pray – Amen."

Welcome into the family! You are now entitled to all of the promises in scripture, including those we are discussing now. Make sure you become part of a church that will teach you more about the Word of God.

So the million dollar question is this; "Can a believer who has been made free by Christ, be in bondage?" The answer is yes! Galatians 5:13 (NLT) says *"For you have been called to live in freedom, my brothers and sisters. But don't use your freedom to satisfy your sinful nature. Instead, use your freedom to serve one another in love"*. Because freedom gives us the authority to choose the course of our own lives, we can choose certain lifestyles or patterns that lead to unhealthy, ungodly and unproductive practices that perpetuate addictions and/or bondage. This explains why we have so many believers hooked on the various vices we see in the world today. It's not because they have not been made free, it's because they chose to use that freedom to satisfy the lust of the flesh – which, by the way, will never be satisfied.

But here's the ten-million dollar question, "When a believer's choice has led to a life of bondage, does that negate or cause that believer to no longer be free?" The answer is emphatically NO, because freedom is not based on your situation, it is based on an empowerment from the Lord Jesus Christ. That gives the believer the right to choose to change the course of their life regardless of current circumstances. This means we never lose our authority or freedom to choose to get out; even when it was our choices that got us in.

If you're addicted to porn, drugs, alcohol, gambling, eating or whatever; freedom gives you the authority to choose to break that area of bondage. You may need to choose to go into rehab, receive deliverance, join a support group, get under a doctor's care, change your relationships – the point is, freedom allows you to make the necessary choices to get free and stay free. Please note, freedom won't make you do anything but it does guarantee you will always have the authority to make choices that line up with God's Word and will for your life. This will ultimately determine the quality of life you live. John 10:10 tells us that Christ came that we may have life and have it more abundantly. The problem is most believers see this as a guarantee of an abundant life, but it is actually the guarantee of the *opportunity* for an abundant life. One that did not exist before Christ came and made us free.

This means the abundant life is not an automatic occurrence that you can just pray for, fast for, or wait for. On the contrary, it's the promise of an opportunity to use your freedom to align yourself with the will of God in order to live the abundant life that is God's will for you. Again, this lack of understanding has many believers frustrated. They're waiting on an outcome that is not guaranteed instead of maximizing the opportunity (freedom) that is in fact the guarantee. As we know maximized opportunities are not predicated on circumstances, but on our capacity to make the right choices in the circumstances. This leads us back to the powerful role freedom plays in the life of a believer.

To help you get a better understanding of freedom let's briefly examine three reasons God sets the believer free. In Exodus 10:3 Moses tells Pharaoh to let God's people go that they may serve Him. The first reason for freedom is to serve God. After all, God says we can't serve two masters so God had to free them from Pharaoh to give them a choice to serve Him. The second reason scripture gives for freedom is to serve one another as we read earlier in Galatians 5:13. The final reason is to fulfill purpose or do the good works which is referenced in Ephesians 2:8-10. Having this understanding that all believers have been made free to serve God, serve one another and fulfill purpose, one must wonder why so many believers are frustrated and living in captivity? We know God is capable and credible to fulfill His Word so the problem must lie with us. I believe the answer to this perpetual problem lies in John 8:31-32 which I call the empowering path to freedom. I believe these verses contain five steps or principles that are critical in fortifying the believer's ability to identify and eliminate negative patterns, lifestyles and habitual behaviors. Those things will keep you bound and stagnant in your pursuit of a victorious life in Christ. Let's look at the scripture again in the MKJV and underline the empowering path to freedom.

John 8:31 *Then Jesus said to the Jews who believed on Him, If you continue in My Word, you are My disciples indeed.* [32] *And you shall know the truth, and the truth shall make you free.* As you can see from the underlined text, the five keys in the empowering path to freedom are, faith in God, abiding in the Word of God, and becoming a disciple of God. Gaining a personal revelation of the person and power of God, which leads to the proper appreciation and application of the empowerment from God, that is freedom.

- 4 -

Believe, Have Faith in God:

The word 'believe' in the above verse is the Greek word "pisteuo" which means "to have faith in, to entrust or to put trust with". Our contextual definition is simply "to come to know and believe in the credibility and capability of God". Faith, or believing in God, is an important key in every aspect of your relationship with Christ and the quality of life you ultimately live. Roman 10:9 tells us that salvation comes through faith. Matthew 9:27-30 says our ability to receive from God is based on our level of faith. 1 John 5:1-5 tells us that the only way we can overcome the world and its vices is by faith. We can see why faith or the belief in God is the first and most critical step on the empowering path to freedom.

Continuing/Abiding in the Word of God:

The word 'continue' comes from the Greek word "meno" which means "to stay in a given place or state, to abide, dwell, remain and stand". Our contextual definition is "to diligently pursue and abide in the Word of God". When you truly believe in God and His Word there should be a consistent pursuit of that which you say you believe in. This enables you to learn to live by the Word of God and abide in the presence of God because you have made the decision to stay in pursuit of God.

Becoming a Disciple of God:

The word 'disciple' refers to a person who has willfully become a learner, or pupil of God by way of developing an intimate personal and positional relationship with God with a focus on being changed into His likeness. This typically happens by moving through the stages of observer, follower, student and ultimately a practitioner. The goal of a disciple, as observed in scripture, is to live a life that produces the same level and likeness of manifestation as Jesus. This is what Jesus meant in John 14:12 when He said *"Verily, verily, I say unto you, He that believeth on me, the works that I do shall he do also; and greater works than these shall he do; because I go unto my Father"*.

And You Shall Know the Truth - Gaining a Personal Revelation of the Person and Power of God:

Biblical truth, in and of itself, does not change. It is the unmovable foundation that every believer's life should be built on. However, biblical truth that's revealed but not internalized by the believer becomes information that produces no real manifestation in your life. This is why knowing the truth or having a heartfelt, life changing conviction of the truth usually comes after making the decision to have faith in God, abide in the word of God, and be a practitioner (disciple) of the ways of God. Truth then becomes two-fold in your life. There is the internal awareness that the God you believe, pursue, and pattern your life after is who He says He is and can do all that His word says He can do. That understanding of truth also brings the awareness that you are who God said you are and you can do all that God said you can do. At this point the words in scripture are no longer just words, they are the way, the truth and the light that will set you free to become everything scripture says you are.

Freedom:

As I mentioned earlier freedom won't make you do anything, but it will release you to live the abundant life Christ made available. Even though this life is available to all who accept Jesus Christ as Lord and Savior it will only be maximized by those who choose to use that freedom to serve God, each other and fulfill the purpose you were created, ordained and set free to fulfill.

Chapter Two:

God is in Control and Without Limits

*Yours, O LORD, is the greatness, the power, the glory,
the victory, and the majesty. Everything in the heavens
and on earth is yours, O LORD, and this is your kingdom.
We adore you as the one who is over all things.* [12] *Wealth
and honor come from you alone, for you rule over
everything. Power and might are in your hand, and at
your discretion people are made great and given strength.*
1Chronicles 29:11-12 (NLT)

Right from the beginning I want to emphasize the importance of believing and knowing that God is in control and without limits. It would be impossible for a believer to have unlimited faith in a God that you believed had limitations. So the first critical and empowering step in breaking free from bondage and maintaining freedom from all negative patterns, mindsets and habitual behaviors; is the revelation that God is bigger than you and all of your challenges. He is even bigger than those seemingly insurmountable obstacles that you may be facing right now in your life.

Bondage occurs in the life of the believer when the ability to break free and stay free from an undesirable pattern of behavior has been lost. At that point your only hope for deliverance is to get assistance from someone who is stronger than you and your bondage. It would take someone who has the authority and ability to empower you to not only resist the trappings of your problem, but also to establish or reestablish authority in that area of your life.

In my case, I had tried for years to overcome my addictions

without long-term success. Over time, those repeated failures brought me to the conclusion that I was not strong enough on my own to get free and stay free. Sure, I had won some battles by staying clean for three months, six months and even a whole year. But once the circumstances of my life made me too sad, too happy, too tired, too angry, too weak or too anything for that matter, I would fall back again. I realized that will power was only as strong as the source willing the power. And as long as I depended on myself to be that source of power, I was inadvertently setting myself up for another fall.

Once we understand that God is the source behind all of the power that exists, we can also understand that God has the authority and ability to transfer portions of His power, might and strength unto us. In 1Chronicles 29:11-12 we are shown that the strength we need to overcome our challenges is made available to us through our relationship with God, thereby equipping us, through God, for complete victory in Him. It is only through God that we can gain the strength we need to overcome every obstacle that we face.

The Power of God

In Deuteronomy 4:39, the scripture tells us that we should take the time to consider (by observation and evaluation) in the innermost parts of our being, that God is God and there is no other. In order for you to have a realistic expectation for perpetual deliverance and victory in every area of your life, you must clearly understand that the God you serve is in control and without limits.

Know therefore this day, and consider it in thine heart, that the Lord He is God in heaven above and upon the earth beneath: there is none else. Deuteronomy 4:39

It is important for you to settle the matter of who is really in control once and for all, because your ongoing success depends on your confidence in the power of God. Believe me, the devil and your flesh will challenge you on this one, so let's make sure you are grounded in this truth straight from the Word of God. Colossians 1:16-17 says *"For by him were all things created, that are in heaven, and that are in earth, visible and invisible, whether they be thrones, or dominions, or principalities, or powers all things were created by him, and for him And he is before all things, and by him all things consist"*

This testifies that everything in heaven and on earth, things we can see and things we can't see, were all created by God, work for God, and only continue to exist because God allows it. This clearly shows us that God is in control of what was, what is and all that will ever be. When we look at creation unfolding in the book of Genesis 1:1-2, we can begin to see the depth of God's inexhaustible power and all-knowing nature. When we look at creation we can clearly see God did not start with a model or an example to follow. There was no green grass in place or abandoned neighborhoods to rebuild. There were no architectural floor plans, no tools, no construction workers or warehouses full of world-creating supplies just waiting on God to place His order. God saw nothing that would indicate promise or potential as His Spirit was hovering over the vast nothing that we now call Earth.

First this*: God created the Heavens and Earth—all you see, all you don't see. Earth was a soup of nothingness, a bottomless emptiness, an inky blackness. God's Spirit brooded like a bird above the watery abyss.* Genesis 1:1-2 (MSG)

The first of the two, often overlooked, attributes that reinforce the power of God I want to briefly focus on is foresight. Foresight is the ability to look forward or have a view of the future and then to care for and lay aside provisions for future needs. Foresight gives God the ability to look at nothing and see something. It also produces the capability to identify future challenges based on current conditions. Through foresight, God has the wherewithal to make plans and provisions for things which have not yet come to pass. Think about everything that would ever need to happen in order for God's plan for the sun to continue to shine and for the earth to continue to be a life-sustaining source. God was able to see it and address it clearly before the beginning of time. This is why God never had to send out a repairman to jump-start the moon or re-adjust the sun, because He could see at the beginning all that would ever need to be addressed.

What do you think is more important to God: the earth, or His children for whom the earth was created to sustain? Well, the answer is, His children. If you have accepted Christ as your Lord and Savior, you are a child of God, recreated by God, and should therefore personalize the benefits of God's foresight for your life. To help you really get this, take a minute to internalize and personalize this statement: "God has a plan for my life." Next say the following out loud with boldness:

"Before God created me, He saw all my tomorrows. He knew every test, trial, temptation and challenge I would ever face in this life; and nothing that I am going through right now is a surprise to God. Therefore, the provision for my victory must already be in place."

The second attribute is what I call "Self-Contained Resources." Resources are defined as a source of supply, support or capability in dealing with a situation. In essence, resources are the means to a desired end. Scripture tells us that every resource God needed for creation was fully contained in Him and brought into existence through the power of His spoken word. This means God doesn't need any outside help. Again, when we personalize this, we see that our God is capable and credible to do everything He promised in His Word; regardless of current situations or circumstances. Now, let's continue to prove that God is in control and without limits by focusing on His supremacy.

God: The Only Supreme Being

Now search all of history, from the time God created people on the earth until now, and search from one end of the heavens to the other. Has anything as great as this ever been seen or heard before? [33]Has any nation ever heard the voice of God speaking from fire—as you did—and survived? [34]Has any other god dared to take a nation for himself out of another nation by means of trials, miraculous signs, wonders, war, a strong hand, a powerful arm, and terrifying acts? Yet that is what the LORD your God did for you in Egypt, right before your eyes. [35]"He showed you these things so you would know that the LORD is God and there is no other. Deuteronomy 4:32-35 (NLT)

Who is like you among the gods, O LORD—glorious in holiness, awesome in splendor, performing great wonders?
Exodus 15:11 (NLT)

Supreme, by definition, is highest in rank or authority; paramount, chief or ultimate. Or, you could simply say that God has unmatched power and authority. You have to wrap your mind around the fact that nothing is bigger, better, stronger or smarter than God. God is God all by Himself. As we can see in the scriptures above, God is the designer, creator and ultimate authority in heaven and on earth. To help you get a clearer understanding of the supremacy of God, let's take a look at three key factors.

Factor #1- Nothing can compare to God

In order to make a true comparison, you must have something that is similar in appearance, value, capability and or authority. The Bible makes it very clear that nothing short of man, whom God created in His image, can be remotely compared to God.

Ponder Point: When we evaluate and observe what God has accomplished on Earth, we witness God's unmatched supernatural abilities and demonstrated acts of power! This makes it very clear that nothing has earned the right to be compared to God based on merit, accomplishment or displayed acts of power.

Factor #2 - Nothing can compete with God

As with making a comparison, when you think about competition, you need to have two or more entities that have the same or similar talents, power and abilities in order for the challenge to actually be competitive. If one team is bigger, stronger, faster and better than the other team, they can still play the game; it just will not be competitive because the lesser team won't have a realistic chance to win. Deuteronomy 3:24 (ESV) speaks directly to this point when we read, *O Lord GOD, you have only begun to show your servant your greatness and your mighty hand. For what god is there in heaven or on earth who can do such works and mighty acts as yours?* We see this point further magnified in Nahum 1:7-9 (NLT) *The LORD is good, a strong refuge when trouble comes. He is close to those who trust in him. [8]But he will sweep away his enemies in an overwhelming flood. He will pursue his foes into the darkness of night. [9]Why are you scheming against the LORD? He will destroy you with one blow; he won't need to strike twice!*

God's power and authority has been challenged throughout history and the results are documented in the scriptures. Beginning with satan; who challenged God and was cast out of heaven through Pharaoh who challenged God and was destroyed with His army in the Red Sea. Although these were real challenges, they were never competitive because God was never in jeopardy of losing, because God is infinitely greater than all who would oppose His ultimate authority.

Ponder Point: God is not a source of power. He is the power source! Therefore all power that exists in heaven and on earth exists because God allows it.

Factor #3 - Nothing can circumvent the power or plan of God.

When we look at the life of Joseph we see this truth played out in scripture. Starting in Genesis 37, God gives the seventeen-year-old Joseph a dream that indicates His plan for Joseph's life. Although Joseph is excited about God's plan, others around him are not. Consequently, his brothers put him into a pit, sold him to Midianite merchants, who in turn sold him into slavery in Egypt. While a slave in Egypt, God gave Joseph favor with his master, Potiphar, who appointed Joseph to be his personal assistant in charge of his house and all his property. This good fortune was short lived, as Joseph was falsely accused of a crime and thrown into prison. While in prison God gave Joseph favor with the jailer who put him in charge of the other prisoners. Years go by but God's plan for Joseph is unaltered. Finally, God gives Joseph the answer to the king's recurring dream. Now, at age thirty and against all worldly odds, Joseph is promoted Governor over all of Egypt. It took thirteen long years of pain, persecution, and overcoming obstacles, but God's plan ultimately prevailed.

Through the story of Joseph we learn that success is not predicated on the position of others when it has already been determined by the providential plan and power of God. This is why we can count it to be truth, *"If God is for us, who can be against us?"* Romans 8:31-b

---

Ponder Point: No person, no place, no thing, no power and no devil can stop God from fulfilling His plan and purpose for your life.

The Person of God: God is a God of Love

1 John 4:8,16 reminds us that the very nature and essence of God is love. This must be internalized because if we cannot comprehend this truth, we will never be able to cultivate and have confidence in the relationship that God desires to have with us, His children. Let's look at three key characteristics of how God demonstrates and validates His love for us in ways that can clearly be seen.

1. <u>God's Love is Unconditional.</u>

This is very hard for most adults to understand because most, if not all of our relationships have had strings attached. People generally give with the expectation of getting something in return and if we don't comply we usually feel the wrath of their pain and disappointment.

God's ways are not our ways. Therefore, we must break the habit of relating to God based on the relationships we have had with others. God is not like us and if we don't get this we will never be able to fully receive God's love because we will see ourselves as undeserving and unable to meet what we perceive to be God's expectations for us. Romans 5:7-8 (NLT) tells us *"Now, most people would not be willing to die for an upright person, though someone might perhaps be willing to die for a person who is especially good. ⁸But God showed his great love for us by sending Christ to die for us while we were still sinners."*

God does not give with the expectation of getting something in return. God gives because He loves us and wants to supply and furnish us with everything we need to live the abundant life that He sent Jesus to make available. This is what John 3:16 means when it says *"For God so loved the world, that he gave his only begotten Son, that whosoever believeth in him should not perish, but have everlasting life."*

Ponder Point: we did nothing to earn God's love and we can do nothing to lose God's love because God's love is unconditional.

---

2. God's love knows no boundaries.

Romans 8:35,38-39 (AMP) starts by asking this question, *"Who shall ever separate us from Christ's love? Shall suffering and affliction and tribulation? Or calamity and distress? Or persecution or hunger or destitution or peril or sword?... ³⁸For I am persuaded beyond doubt (am sure) that neither death nor life, nor angels nor principalities, nor things impending and threatening nor things to come, nor powers, ³⁹Nor height nor depth, nor anything else in all creation will be able to separate us from the love of God which is in Christ Jesus our Lord."*

Scripture tells us that nothing can separate us from the love of God, including the things we did or continue to do that makes us feel bad or unlovable. God knew you were going to do it before the foundation of the world yet He chose to love you anyway. God's love does not give us permission to stay in our sin, on the contrary it gives us grace, mercy, and the power we need to get out and stay out.

Ponder Point: Our highest highs or lowest lows cannot put us out of the reach of God's love. Don't focus on where you've been, or where you are, just remember God's love is there with you and will continue to sustain you while empowering you to be free.

3.   God's love is personal and paternal.

As a parent, I have seen my children make many mistakes. Though I have been disappointed and at times angry, I have never stopped loving them or desiring the best for their lives. Likewise, I remember when I got clean from drugs, I bought my mother a new watch hoping it would ease her pain and prove my commitment to do right by replacing the watch I had stolen and sold while using drugs. I'm not sure what I was expecting her to say or do, but she just looked at me and said "The watch is nice, but the best gift you can give me is to give yourself a chance to have a good life. That will be the greatest gift I could ever ask for". Praise God that twenty-four years and many gifts later, she has watched God transform my life beyond both of our wildest dreams. My point is this; the love a parent has for a child is the closest example we have of the love that God has for us. Although this is a good example, it still pales in comparison to the all-encompassing love of God.

Ponder Point: God's love is not abstract. It is intimate, personal and purposeful. God created you. God knows you. God loves you and wants to help you grow in Him so that you may become the person He created you to be.

God our Provider

God demonstrates His love for us by consistently making provision for every situation or need we will ever encounter. This may sound foundational, but surprisingly many believers have failed to internalize this truth. Until this is completely understood you will not be able to stop relying on yourself or others and rely solely on God. God is the only unfailing and totally reliable source that exists. This explains why relying on anything other than God, can only produce temporary relief at best. We may want to do right and others might really want to help us do right, but because we are neither omnipotent nor omniscient, there are limits to what we can do on our own.

Let's consider breathing. Because breathing is such a natural occurrence we think of it as being automatic. But the Bible reminds us that every breath we take that pumps life into our body is a gift provided by God and something that could not happen without His grace. If man does not have the ability to sustain his own life; he surely does not have the ability on his own to provide the additional elements needed to make that life productive.

To help me really get this revelation, the Holy Spirit gave me what I now call the "Sole Source Test." The Holy Spirit had me write down everything I felt I needed from God to have what I considered an abundant life. I came up with words like love, strength, protection, health, money, etc. Then I was directed to go to the scriptures and see if God had already supplied these provisions in His word. You probably know the answer, but I will share a portion of my findings with you as biblical proof. They can also be used as a reference when you take the sole source test yourself. The words and phrases below are the exact words or related words that I came up with. The scripture references are the biblical proof that God is the provider of everything we will ever need.

William's Sole Source Test Results:

- God is my source of life and health.

Neither is He served by human hands, as though He lacked anything, for it is He Himself Who gives life and breath and all things to all (people). Acts 17:25 (AMP)

- God is my source of wisdom, protection, favor, and all good things.

For the LORD God is a sun and shield: the LORD will give grace and glory: no good thing will he withhold from them that walk uprightly. Psalm 84:11

- God is my source of every good and perfected gift and my foundation for stability.

Every good gift and every perfect gift is from above, and cometh down from the Father of lights, with whom is no variableness, neither shadow of turning. James 1:17

- God is the source of my strength and protection. He is my place of refuge.

The LORD is my rock, and my fortress, and my deliverer; my God, my strength, in whom I will trust; my buckler, and the horn of my salvation, and my high tower. Psalm 18:2

- God is my buffer against insurmountable temptation and provider of escape.

No temptation has taken you but what is common to man; but God is faithful, who will not allow you to be tempted above what you are able, but with the temptation also will make a way to escape, so that you may be able to bear it. 1Corinthians 10:13 (MKJV)

- God is my source of adequate sufficiency for all situations.

And he said unto me, My grace is sufficient for thee: for my strength is made perfect in weakness. Most gladly therefore will I rather glory in my infirmities, that the power of Christ may rest upon me. 2Corinthians 12:9

- God is my source of peace.

Peace I leave with you, my peace I give unto you: not as the world giveth, give I unto you. Let not your heart be troubled, neither let it be afraid. John 14:27

- God is the foundation of my faith.

I have told you these things, so that in Me you may have [perfect] peace and confidence. In the world you have tribulation and trials and distress and frustration; but be of good cheer [take courage; be confident, certain, undaunted]! For I have overcome the world. [I have deprived it of power to harm you and have conquered it for you.] John 16:33 (AMP)

- God is the originator of my inheritance, my rescuer from satan, the payer of my ransom and the forgiver of my sins.

Giving thanks to the Father, Who has qualified and made us fit to share the portion which is the inheritance of the saints (God's holy people) in the Light. [13] [The Father] has delivered and drawn us to Himself out of the control and the dominion of darkness and has transferred us into the kingdom of the Son of His love, [14] In Whom we have our redemption through His blood, [which means] the forgiveness of our sins. Colossians 1:12-14 (AMP)

- God is my source of healing.

But he was wounded for our transgressions, he was bruised for our iniquities: the chastisement of our peace was upon him; and with his stripes we are healed. Isaiah 53:5

- God is my source of prosperity (spiritual, soulish and financially).

Both riches and honor come from You, and You reign over all. In Your hands are power and might; in Your hands it is to make great and to give strength to all. 1Chronicles 29:12 (AMP)

The blessing of the LORD, it maketh rich, and he addeth no sorrow with it. Proverbs 10:22

Sole Source Test

Instructions: Make a list of the things you consider necessary to have an abundant life. Next search in your Bible's concordance for scriptures that contain the exact or related words you chose. This will help you to identify God's promises that are related to the items on your list and this is also an excellent way to study your Bible and increase your faith. For example:

- What do I feel I need from God?

  I need to be able to live without being tormented by FEAR

- God's provision for that need:

For God hath not given us the spirit of fear; but of power, and of love, and of a sound mind. 2 Timothy 1:7

This tells me first of all that the fear I have did not come from God (so I probably need to give it back to who I got it from). Second, it tells me that God has given me the power, character and intellectual capacity to override that fear and replace it with faith.

After reviewing my results and taking your own Sole Source Test, you should clearly see that God is the provider of everything you will ever need. Once you get this revelation internalized, you will start seeking direction from God in every area of your life. Let's briefly focus on an area of God's provision that I feel is critical for all believers - especially those of us who have experienced repeated defeat in specific areas of our lives.

God is our Deliverer

And he said, The LORD is my rock, and my fortress, and my deliverer 2Samuel 22:2

To make sure you fully understand the ramifications of deliverance let's examine three definitions for deliver.

Hebrew Definition ~ Deliverer – palat, pronounced paw-lat - to bring into security, to cause to escape, cast forth or to bring to safety. Brown-Driver-Briggs Hebrew definitions published in 1906 public domain.

<u>Contextual Definition</u> ~ Deliverer – "A supernatural act of God wherein He meets an individual in the midst of their bondage, pulls them into His presence, and fills them with His power, causing the believer to live free from the bondage of their flesh and the devil."

<u>Personal Definition</u> ~ Delivered - I don't have to use _____ (fill in the blank) when I don't want to, but more importantly I don't have to use it when I do want to.

Although my personal definition of delivered may sound simple to you, believe me - this revelation changed my life. During the first few years after I had stopped using, even though I felt in my heart that God had delivered me from the bondage of drugs and alcohol, I wasn't able to fully receive it because the urge to use was still there. I believed the urges were an indicator that I had not been fully delivered. So God, through the Holy Spirit, had to show me that my deliverance was not predicated on the urges, but on my newfound ability through God to resist them. This was my turning point. I finally realized that deliverance didn't necessarily mean I would never want to use drugs again. Instead, it meant I would never have to use them again regardless of how I felt or how strong the urges were - even at those times when my mind, body and the enemy were telling me I would not be able to resist.

I am Godly proud to say that at the time of this writing, it has been nearly twenty-four years since I have used drugs or alcohol. Yet, there are still times when I get the urge to use. It's during those times that I simply confess that I am delivered, submit myself to my deliverer, resist the enemy and the urges go away. Always remember, when God delivers you He actually meets you where you are, pulls you into His presence, fills you with His power and gives you the authority to resist the things that you could not resist on your own. It's important that we always remember we can *"Stand fast therefore in the liberty wherewith Christ hath made us free, and be not entangled again with the yoke of bondage."* Galatians 5:1 *"If the Son therefore shall make you free, ye shall be free indeed"*. John 8:36

<u>Three Focus Points on Deliverance</u>

1. Deliverance from the powers of satan

Ephesians 2 tells us that before we accepted Jesus as our Lord and Savior we were trapped in worldliness, subjected to the power and direction of Satan; a prisoner of the lust of our flesh with no hope of escape on our own. Colossians 1:12-13 tells us that God the Father, through His Son Jesus, delivered us out of the dominion and power of darkness by rescuing us from Satan, breaking the hold sin had over our lives and reconnecting us to God. This means that the devil no longer has any real authority over our lives. He can still try to trick, tempt and test us, but he no longer has the authority to take us anywhere we aren't willing to go. Deliverance means you always have the right and power to refuse to participate.

Remember, victory or defeat is never about the level of opposition. It's always determined by your level of submission to the power and truth contained in the Word of God. You can win against the devil every time if you are willing to *"Submit yourselves therefore to God. Resist the devil, and he will flee from you"*. James 4:7

Ponder Point: God has delivered us out of the dominion and power of darkness. We now have the ability to live free because the choice to succeed or fail has been given back to us.

---

2. Deliverance from the inability to resist our flesh

The Bible tells us that our flesh never changes. By nature, it will never be a willing participant in our spiritual endeavors because it will always seek to please itself. So when we accept Jesus as our Lord and Savior, our spirit man is renewed. We are born again, giving us the ability through Christ to override the carnal desires of our flesh and resist the attacks of the enemy.

No temptation has taken you but what is common to man; but God is faithful, who will not allow you to be tempted above what you are able, but with the temptation also will make a way to escape, so that you may be able to bear it 1Corinthians 10:13 (MKJV)

Ponder Point: Don't wait on your flesh to get in agreement or to feel good about your decision to serve God because that will never happen. Even though your flesh might try to make you think otherwise, remember that it ultimately works for you and can be controlled by you.

3. Deliverance from the attacks, persecutions, and afflictions brought on by others

Contrary to what some might think, being a Christian does not remove us from harm's way. In truth, it's the standing up for our beliefs that are often the cause of the attacks and persecutions we experience. However, Psalm 34:19 tells us *"Many are the afflictions of the righteous: but the LORD delivereth him out of them all."* As believers we should always remind ourselves that we are never alone, we will never be exposed to more than we can handle and God will deliver us out of it all.

God our Restorer

I can't begin to tell you what the negative lifestyles, patterns and self-defeating behaviors have cost me in the past. The devil had me convinced that everything I lost, had stolen or given away could never be recovered. I really believed that the dreams, visions and prophetic words I had received were lost and that my best hope for internal fulfillment was to learn how to handle setbacks, disappoints, defeats and lack with grace.

At that point in my life the devil had me right where he wanted me. I was a believer without much faith, hope or expectation for an abundant life. Think about it, if the devil can minimize your expectations he also minimizes your effort, which simultaneously minimizes the outcomes in every situation. When you don't expect much - you don't do much, and when you don't do much, you get just what you expect - not much.

In order to change your expectations you must first change what you believe to be true as it relates to your situation. As believers it's important that we train ourselves not to receive anything as truth if we cannot validate it in scripture. We can't depend on what we feel, think, hear or even see to be the truth. We must live by the Word of God. So let's go to the Word now and reestablish proper expectations by establishing God as our restorer.

To restore is bring back to a former, original or normal condition; to bring back to a state of health, soundness or vigor, or to put back to a former place, position or rank. Simply said, to restore is to get back something that has been taken away, given away or lost.

Two Focus Points on Restoration

1. Recover

We see in the following verses, God can recover what was stolen from you by force. But we also see the pattern, process, and mindset that should be followed. When you read 1Samuel 30, you should note that when David's camp was overrun by the enemy and his family taken hostage he didn't just get mad, fly into a rage and take off after his enemy. David was systematic and followed a four-step process that I believe we all should learn and implement in our own lives. If you are not already familiar with this story you should take the time now to read 1Samuel 30:1-8 and then let's look at the four-step process David followed.

Step One: Encourage - 1Samuel 30:4 *David and the people with him lifted up their voice and wept, until they had no more power to weep.* A loss can produce great pain in our lives. But we really need to look at the, "what you do next" factor. Once a situation and its impact have been properly understood, we can see that the most important thing is what we do next. Let me be clear, David felt the pain and reacted to the pain, but he quickly realized he would not be able to respond effectively without pulling himself together and focusing on a solution to the problem or the "what you do next" factor. V.6 tells us that David encouraged (strengthened, made firm, resolute or secured) himself in the Lord. David went from being discouraged to encouraged simply by removing his focus from the problem and placing it on the problem solver.

Step Two: Inquire of the Lord - David didn't try to guess or figure out what he should do; he prayed. For believers there should never be a time when we don't know what to do. We may not know what action we should take next. but we should always know what to do. We must pray (inquire) and seek God's word, direction and desired outcome for our situation. Then when God tells you what to do, submit yourself to His authority and comply. By doing so, you hand over your concern to Him, and it becomes His responsibility to bring His desired outcome to pass in your situation.

Step Three: Establish - David established a plan of action based on the revealed Word of God.

Step Four: Execute - Because David followed through on the plan of God it produced the purposes of God in His situation; he recovered all.

2. Return

*And I will restore to you the years that the locust hath eaten, the cankerworm, and the caterpillar, and the palmerworm, my great army which I sent among you. *[26]*And ye shall eat in plenty, and be satisfied, and praise the name of the LORD your God, that hath dealt wondrously with you: and my people shall never be ashamed. *[27]*And ye shall know that I am in the midst of Israel, and that I am the LORD your God, and none else: and my people shall never be ashamed.* Job 2:25-27

If my people, which are called by my name, shall humble themselves, and pray, and seek my face, and turn from their wicked ways; then will I hear from heaven, and will forgive their sin, and will heal their land. 2Chronicles 7:14

Part of God's process of restoration is to cause a return in your life. My contextual definition for return in context with the two scriptures above is "to receive back what was forfeited because of sin, rebellion, the lack of willingness to maintain Godly standards and/or poor decisions made on the part of the believer".

This means the fact that you made mistakes does not mean you have to miss out on fulfilling purpose and reaching destiny. God can redeem the time for the years you have lost by restoring you spiritually, emotionally, physically and financially and by accelerating you on your destiny's path. God says in His Word when you turn back to Him, acknowledge and correct your error, He will hear from heaven, forgive your sin, heal your land and remove your shame and guilt. Glory be to God.

Ponder Point: When you truly understand the love of God, it gives you complete confidence that the power of God is consistently being exerted on your behalf.

I am certain that some of you reading this book right now are thinking that you already knew most, if not all of the material I have covered thus far. Yet despite having that knowledge, you're still struggling with negative lifestyles, patterns and habitual behaviors. Before you start to lose hope, remember that we've only just begun and there are five more key truths to explore in the coming chapters. But to stay in the moment, let me give you five observations on the common reasons believers continue to experience defeat while understanding that God is in control.

- They don't really want to stop or change.

These believers are looking for a better, easier, or a less painful way that does not require them to stop the sin or the negative behavior completely. They want to continue the behavior by trying to figure out a way to manage or minimize the pain, guilt and shame it causes. They don't want to close the door and throw away the key because they have not made the decision that no matter what, they are not going back into the sinful or unproductive behavior.

- They are not seeking God.

This is the "I believe I can still figure this thing out on my own" mentality. This is always destined to fail, because this person forgot it was their figuring that got them in trouble in the first place. In this case their pride keeps them from admitting they need help from God and others God will send.

- They are seeking God without a willingness to do what He says.

This is the "It doesn't take all that" mentality. These believers are looking to have hands laid on them, get all tingly, hit the floor, get up, and never have a desire to sin again. They want to get free without doing any ongoing work to stay free. Remember, we don't get to decide what it takes to be free. We only get to decide if we're willing to do what it takes.

- They have not fully internalized the forgiving, delivering power of God available to them.

In many cases these believers can be in faith for others, but because of guilt and shame from their past, they struggle to believe that God will do for them what they see Him doing for others. This is because they have not internalized and personalized God's love for them.

- Simply have not made the commitment to give their lives completely over to God

This believer has one foot in the world and one foot in the Word and is still trying to serve two masters. The decision to totally submit/commit to God has not yet been made, therefore every temptation presents a new decision that has to be made in the heat of the situation or temptation. For example, you have not made the decision to completely submit to the will of God for your life, and someone drops a dollar in front of you. Well, the decision will most likely be easy for you to tell the person they dropped a dollar. But, what if they dropped one hundred dollars and you were broke. Now you have to decide what to do, on the spot, while considering your current state of lack and need. This is a set up for a disaster. The point I want you to understand is this, once you submit totally there is not a new decision to make because your decision is not based on the situation, it is based on your submission to God. Therefore you don't make new decisions; you just take the actions that validate the decision that has already been made. This reduces confusion, minimizes temptation, takes your flesh out of play and produces repeated actions that are pleasing to God, productive for you and are repeatable patterns for success.

Chapter Reflection and Meditation

Invest some time to see which of the five statements above describe you. Be honest with yourself in determining why you struggle in that area. Seek God's word and wisdom to help you overcome that important, initial barrier. Examine yourself to decide if you're ready to commit totally to the process of change. Understand that this may be one of the hardest things you have ever done and that there will be certain aspects of your life you need to give up or change forever. Meditate Colossians 1:13, 16-17, 1Chronicles 29:12, and 2Corinthians 12:9. Write down what the Holy Spirit reveals to you about yourself and how these verses can be applied in empowering you to live free from bondage.

Chapter Three:

Self-Discovery – Seeing Yourself Through the Word of God

And God said, Let us make man in our image,
after our likeness: and let them have dominion
over the fish of the sea, and over the fowl of the
air, and over the cattle, and over all the earth,
and over every creeping thing that creepeth
upon the earth.   Genesis. 1:26

We now know that the first part of building a foundation for your Christian walk is to believe, then know that God is in control and without limits. The second part is to develop an accurate vision of yourself based on your relationship with God.

Everyone has a personal image of himself or herself. We all see ourselves in a certain way. This vision that we have of ourselves, whether it's right or wrong, will determine our personal expectations for success or failure in life. This is critical because our expectations determine the quality of our decisions, as well as the amount of effort we will exert toward bringing those decisions to pass. Our efforts, coupled with the quality of our decisions, will always impact the outcome of our lives.

In all of our relationships, whether we admit it or not, we generally treat others based on our perception of what kind of person we feel they are. This is not judging them; it's simply identifying our perception of them. This is very important to understand because no matter what your perception may be, it will be a factor in your interactions with that person. For example, imagine you have a relationship with someone you perceive to be a gossip. Even if you had no evidence to support your perceptions, you would intentionally limit the amount of personal information you share with that person.

The point is this; we act a certain way toward others and toward ourselves based on what we perceive to be true. So the critical question is this: Are we looking at ourselves based on our personal perceptions, or on our God given potential? Are we seeing ourselves through the eyes of God or through the eyes of our past experiences? God sees us based on who He created us to be, but our personal perspective doesn't actually tell us who we are or who we will become. It is merely a reflection of what we've been through.

As we begin the process of self-discovery we must keep in mind that we are only looking to discover, not define. This may sound new and even strange to some, but until you're able to start seeing (discovering) yourself through the eyes and Word of God, you will always have a flawed and inaccurate image of yourself. Most people act like the person they think they are, because they don't really know who they are. The vision or image they have formed of themselves is based on past experiences and not biblical truths.

God, our creator, is the only one who has the right to decide who we are, what we are, and for what purpose we were created. As believers we don't get to decide who we are. We only get to decide who we act like. So, if you are not seeing yourself through the eyes of God, you have an incorrect view of yourself that is falsely governing your actions and your attitudes relating to yourself. This must be corrected before you will be able to take authority and dominion over your flesh and your circumstances in order to take your rightful place in God's plan and purpose for your life.

Ponder Point: Most people act like who they think they are because they don't know who they really are.

Three Common Mistakes Believers Make While Acquiring an Accurate Barometer in the Discovery Process.

1. Environment

Environment can be defined as the surroundings, conditions, influences or the social and cultural forces that shape the life of a person or a population. The things you see around you can dramatically affect your personal view of self and the expectations you develop for your life. If you were to grow up in a stable, nurturing household where your older siblings went to law school and became successful lawyers, chances are you would expect the same or at least something comparable for yourself. On the contrary, if you grew up in an environment where drugs, alcohol and violence were prevalent, it would be very hard for you to see yourself as one who would break that cycle. It is a proven fact that our environment plays a significant role in how we view ourselves, but it is equally true that our environment doesn't tell us who we are - it just tells us from where we've come.

Most of our standards of living, expectations, and overall views about life and ourselves stem from our environment. We carry these negative or positive views with us wherever we go. Even factors like time and success are generally not strong enough to change these views. It usually takes a real purposeful effort to facilitate change in an area that is so connected to our core being. This is why it is not uncommon to see people who have surpassed expectations by overcoming the terrible environment in which they grew up, act out in self-defeating behaviors that cause them to lose everything they've gained. Though their situations and statuses may have changed, their internal views of self have not changed and therefore still negatively influences their external behavior.

2. Input

Input is the positive and negative information that has been deposited into your life by what you have personally experienced, heard from others or believe to be true about yourself. The self-discovery process is often marred or distorted when we see ourselves based on negative experiences and mistakes from our past, coupled with the negative comments spoken to us or about us from people we view as credible. Many of us still have this negative input stuck in our heads from the things we were told while growing up or in some cases the things we still hear as adults.

In many cases the actual information we currently use in the self-discovery process is that same barrage of negative input that we heard early in our lives. That input was built on other people's opinions without a shred of insight from God. Even if the things they said about you were true or are still true, remember this - the moment you accept Jesus Christ as your Lord and Savior and make a heartfelt decision to stop doing those deeds; those descriptions of you no longer fit.

The day I confessed, repented and made a decision to stop stealing and lying, was the day I stopped calling myself a liar and a thief. Although the full manifestation didn't happen all at once, just changing the image I had of myself to one that lined up with scripture started the process of changing my behavior to line up with what I now believed to be true about myself.

3. Image

The self-image or the picture you have formed of yourself in your mind's eye is generally formed by the environment and input you have received about yourself. This becomes a critical juncture in your life because once you see yourself a certain way, you will respond to what you see. If you see yourself as a failure and make failure your expectation, then chances are you're going to fail. It's important that you truly understand that the image you have of yourself will become the foundation of what you think, and how you think as it pertains to every area of your life. That includes your self-worth and self-esteem. This becomes the determining factor of whether you will feel adequate or inadequate, worthy or unworthy. Will you feel like the victor the Bible says you are, or the victim you may have envisioned yourself to be?

Romans 12:3 tells us not to think more highly of ourselves than we ought. This means we should hold onto an accurate view of ourselves. This is important because the way we view or think about ourselves will impact all of the decisions we make.

Let me be clear, the way you see yourself will dramatically affect the decisions you make about your life, your purpose and your goals. When you think too highly of yourself, you will make decisions based on an expectancy that exceeds your ability and level of maturity. In other words, you will ask for and expect things that you are not mature enough to handle because you have an over-inflated sense of self. This means it is also critical that you don't think lower of yourself than you ought. Which is what I see happening more often in the body of believers. When this is how you view yourself, you will most likely have low self-esteem or low self-value, thus your overall expectations for your quality of life will also be low.

When you don't expect much, you make decisions that are geared to produce just what you expect, not much. If you don't believe that you are who God said you are, then you won't believe that you can do what God said you can do, nor will you believe you can have what God said you can have. The promises God put in His word for you just sit there producing nothing because you don't really believe they are for you.

Although environment, input and self-image are real and impactful components of life, a true and accurate self-assessment can only be found through revelation from God; through His Word.

Ponder Point: What you have experienced does not tell you who you are. It only tells you what you've seen, heard and gone through. The fact that you are still standing is an indicator that there is something in you that is greater than the sum total of all your negative experiences.

God's Word: The Accurate Barometer for Self-Discovery

The foundation of an accurate self-assessment starts at the foundation of the creation of mankind. This is where we see God's original input and intent for our lives. The first thing God put into us was His breath, which contained His DNA. The breath of God doesn't just give us life. It makes us a living soul; able to reason, think, understand, receive wisdom and apply it. This makes man different from anything else God has ever created because it allows us to function like God. God put His DNA in us so the earth could be an extension of heaven by making us an extension of Him in the earth realm. God front-loaded us with everything we would ever need to overcome every obstacle, to recover from every fall and to be a champion in every challenge. God placed into us everything we would ever need to grow, mature, develop and accomplish everything He predestined for us. God put something in us that cannot be duplicated, guarantees success and equips us for victory in every situation. God put His Spirit in us. This means the actual spirit of the living God was deposited into you.

And the LORD God formed man of the dust of the ground, and breathed into his nostrils the breath of life; and man became a living soul. Genesis 2:7

God put His Spirit in us because His original intent was for us to act like Him, look like Him and partner with Him as overseers of all that He created on the earth. God made us the legal guardians, caretakers and rulers over all He owned and gave us the ability, through Him, to continue to produce others like ourselves. He would not have given us this godlike responsibility without first inputting the godlike ability to display His character and excellence, while fulfilling His purpose for our lives.

And God said, Let us make man in our image, after our likeness: and let them have dominion over the fish of the sea, and over the fowl of the air, and over the cattle, and over all the earth, and over every creeping thing that creepeth upon the earth. Genesis 1:26

After looking at the reality of God's original input and intentions for mankind, the question has to be raised: Why is it so difficult to do the things we know God created and equipped us to do? Although this may sound like a hard question, it's actually pretty simple when we go to God's word for the answer. To make sure you have a thorough understanding, we're going to answer the question in two parts. The first part is "Adam's sin and the consequential fall of man." The second part is "Man's lack of diligence in revising his view of his true self."

Adam's Sin and the Fall of Man

Before the fall, Adam did not face the challenges we currently face in life. Adam was born in a perfect environment with a perfect relationship with God. Adam was born wise in his mind, holy in his heart, righteous in his actions, perfect and without flaws. Adam was born into an environment that was untainted and sinless. He had no inherent predispositions, appetites or passions that were contrary to God's plan for him.

The Bible shows that God is a God of choice. God chose to create the heavens and the earth just like He chose to create man in His image and likeness. This means man was created like God, with the ability to choose. God made everything right for Adam to succeed, so it was Adam's choice to fall by choosing to disobey God. Unfortunately, Adam's decision didn't just affect him, it also affected all of mankind. When you read the third chapter of Genesis, you can identify three consequences of Adam's sin that will help us to answer the first part of the question.

Consequence #1 - Death: We clearly see in scripture that Adam did not physically die, he died spiritually. The invisible spirit of God that was originally deposited into Adam that made the presence of God so real and tangible, died in him. Therefore, man's ability to commune with God and function like God also died. This separation destroyed man's potential to fulfill God's purpose by disconnecting man from the God he would need to guide him and empower him to fulfill that purpose.

Consequence #2 - Discomfort: The original privileges and comforts God afforded Adam while living in the Garden of Eden, were eternally lost. Man was evicted from his home, losing access to the perfect environment God had created just for him. It was God's specially prepared place for man. Adam was forced to find a new place to live and grow food from a ground that had been cursed, causing much labor and grief for the durations of his days.

Consequence #3 - Decay: Moral standards were decayed. Man would no longer be born in a perfect environment or born into a right relationship with God. Man would no longer be born with a clean heart and a desire to seek and serve God. Man would now be born into the world with sin in his heart and a desire to please only himself.

Reading Ephesians 2: 1-3,12 gives us additional clarity on man's condition after the fall by using words and phrases that are easy to picture and more vividly describe what we see in today's society. I've identified the main points below for convenience but this is something that warrants additional study on your own.

- Dead: Alive to the world, but dead to God; of no use to God; being incapable of fulfilling the purposes of God.
- Following the course of this world: Doing what everybody else is doing or what feels good to you with no God inspired revelation or Godly vision for your life.
- Under the authority of Satan: Literally, a child of the devil, being forced to follow his mandates and mimic his mindsets.
- Obeying the impulses of the flesh and the thoughts of the mind: Void of the authority or ability to stop engaging in certain behaviors even when you truly want to quit. Chasing instant gratification that needs to be repeated over and over because your flesh never experiences long-term fulfillment or contentment.
- Without Hope: Nothing to look forward to and no reason to believe your life will ever get better.
- Without God: Void of a power that's greater than your source of bondage.

It should be noted that the condition or state of being that we see in Ephesians 2 is not just for unbelievers. V.2 tells us this applies to anyone - saved or unsaved who is careless, rebellious or who goes against the purposes of God. This is something you most definitely should be aware of, especially if you are experiencing any of the conditions noted in the aforementioned scriptures.

The State of Man after Salvation = <u>Saved</u>

For God so loved the world, that he gave his only begotten Son, that whosoever believeth in him should not perish, but have everlasting life. 17 For God sent not his Son into the world to condemn the world; but that the world through him might be saved. John 3:16-17

God fully understood the ramifications of Adam's sin. He knew His children would never be able to take their rightful place as overcomers and conquerors unless they were to be saved from the powers of Satan, the lust of the flesh, and the lure of the world. God sent His only Son, Jesus, so that you and I could be saved.

The word 'saved' comes from the Greek word "sozo," which means "to save, heal, cure, preserve, keep safe and sound, rescued from danger or destruction and delivered". This same word in primitive cultures is translated simply, "to give new life" and "to cause to have a new heart."

My contextual definition for saved is "being delivered, rescued and set free from the evils which have distracted, detoured, diminished and disabled one from receiving and operating in a consistently fruitful relationship with God". Such freedom would enable and empower one to make uninhibited choices and actions to fulfill God's plan and purpose for their life.

The Bible says in 2 Corinthians that once we accept Jesus as our Lord and Savior, old things pass away and all things become new. Yes, you actually become a brand new person. This new you is not based on your environment, past experiences or the image that you currently have of yourself. It has nothing to do with other people's perceptions, past or present mistakes, nor the socio-economic status you currently hold. It is a deposit made into you by God that shifts and changes the nature of your very being.

The word 'new', as it is used here in scripture, comes from the Greek word "Kainos" which means "recently made, fresh, unused, unworn, or a new kind, unprecedented, uncommon or unheard of". You literally become something that is revealed for the first time to yourself and to the world. This new you is empowered by God to display previously unused, unknown and untapped potential and ability that enables you to accomplish a unique and God ordained purpose on this earth.

Before this new you can be fully received and activated, you must allow the old you to pass away. Yes, I did say allow the old you to pass away. We aren't comfortable hearing this because, in most cases, the old is all we know and we have a fear of letting it go. Even though we want a better life, it's often easier to hold on to the old life, than it is to receive something new and unfamiliar.

Let's look briefly at three areas of our new life that are born into existence when we let the old life pass away.

1. The inability to resist: The inability to resist sin, your flesh, Satan, and the lure of the world has passed away. When God saves you, He empowers you with a fresh infusion of His Holy Spirit that enables you to fulfill the purpose He created you to accomplish. Just like Jesus, who being filled with the Holy Spirit and armed with the Word of God, was able to resist sin and Satan, that same Spirit which empowered Jesus, is now alive and active in you.

For we do not have a high priest who cannot be touched with the feelings of our infirmities, but was in all points tempted just as we are, yet without sin. Hebrews 4:15 (MKJV)

For in that He Himself has suffered, having been tempted, He is able to rescue those who are being tempted. Hebrews 2:18 (MKJV)

2. The reestablishing of God's original intent for your life: Your ability to rule and reign is reestablished. You are not just able to resist your flesh, the world and Satan, but now you have power and authority over all three. You can now rebuke the devil, subdue your flesh and command the world to respond to biblical principles spoken in faith. When I first got this revelation, it changed my answer to the commonly asked question, "How is the world treating you?" I used to say things like "It's treating me all right" or "Not too good"; depending on what was going on at the time. Now my answer is, "The world doesn't get to decide how it treats me because my Bible says Jesus overcame the world and gave it to me. Therefore it no longer decides, it responds to my faith-filled demands that line up with scripture."

In order to make sure we have balance on this, let me be clear: the devil and your flesh no longer have authority over you, but they do still have influence. In others words, they can still tempt you, they just can't make you do anything. If you are still stumbling it's not because you don't have authority, it's because you don't fully understand it or have not diligently committed to applying it in every area in your life.

3. A new vision of self: The old vision of yourself should also pass away. You should start to see yourself differently, even when there is no external change that can be seen. You must keep in mind that lasting external change starts on the inside. You will have to decide to change the way you look at yourself, by no longer looking at the former things, but seeing yourself through the Word of God until an outward change becomes visible in your life. For example, the Bible says you are more than a conqueror but you are still struggling with cigarettes. The fact that you are struggling with cigarettes doesn't change who you are, but maintaining the vision of who you are is what empowers you to change what you do.

The question we all have to ask ourselves is this: Is the current vision or picture that we have of ourselves based on who the Bible says we are in 2Corinthians 5:17; or is it based on who we were before we accepted Jesus as Lord as described in Ephesians 2? This leads us into the second part of the answer to our original question: Why is it so difficult to live the life we know God created and equipped us to live? My answer: man's lack of diligence in revising his view of self.

Three Critical Keys in Forming a Bible Based Vision or Image of Self

1. Proper Valuation:

We just read John 3:16, if you don't know your true value or worth, you will most certainly settle for less than God has promised and made available for you, according to His word. Think about it like this; if you were to sell a house that cost you $100,000 to build and someone offered to pay you $1,000,000 for the house, what is the real value of the house? Well, it's actually worth $1,000,000! Although that's not what you paid, the actual value of the house is based on what someone is willing to pay you for it. John 3:16 gives us clarity about our true value or worth by showing us the price that God was willing to pay for us.

God loved us enough to be willing to pay whatever it cost to provide the opportunity for us to be in a right relationship with Him. He already knew that nothing else He had created on earth was valuable enough to pay that price; so the Creator had to sacrifice His only begotten Son for you and I to have an opportunity to re-establish an intimate relationship with Him. The only way you can get an accurate assessment of your true value is to know the price that was paid for you. So if I asked you what you think Jesus is worth, your answer would also determine your own value because Jesus was the price that God paid for you. Take some time to process this because until this fundamental truth has been internalized you will never be able to see or value yourself the way God does.

2. Present Vindication:

Before we accepted Jesus as our Lord and Savior we were bound by a law that said it was our personal responsibility to pay the price for our past, present and future sins. This law also indicated that the price would ultimately be death. We can clearly see in numerous places in scripture that one of the benefits of our relationship with Christ is that we will no longer be required to pay the debt that our sin has racked up. This doesn't provide a reason to continue to sin, but it does provide a release from the pain, guilt and shame our sin has caused us. We no longer have to look at ourselves through the eyes of a sinner. We can now look at ourselves through the eyes of the One who loved us enough to ransom Himself for our rescue. Therefore, the mistakes of our past no longer limit our potential, mitigate our purpose or define our personal expectations for success. They now only serve as a testament and a testimony of the love God has for us.

3. Perpetual Victory:

When taken to heart, 1Corinthians 10:13 reveals two life changing revelations. First, all of the temptations we will ever face are common to man, meaning they are the same tests, trials and temptations that others regularly face and conquer. This means the devil doesn't have a new trick to throw at you, so you don't need to develop a new strategy for success. You just need to know the same biblical principles that have worked for others will also work for you if you apply them with diligence and faith. Secondly, God will not allow the devil to attack you with a temptation, test or trial that God has not already prepared you to handle. In order for me to fully understand this, God had to give me a vision that I will now share with you.

In this vision, the devil was getting ready to attack me, so God looked at the attack, then looked at me and determined that the attack was bigger than what I could handle at that time. God stepped between the attack and myself, preventing it from touching me. My faith, focus and faithfulness had to mature to the point where I would, not only be able to handle the attack, but I would be able to handle it in a way that would display His character and excellence in the process.

Once I locked in on this, I started looking at every situation that I faced as an opportunity to grow, get a victory and bring honor and glory to His name. Please understand, your success is not predicated on the situation. It's predicated on how you respond. Once you see yourself as the one who is guaranteed victory, you will start responding in a way that will produce just what you see, the guaranteed victory.

The Benefits of Having a God Inspired Vision of Self

Where there is no vision, the people cast off restraint; But he that keepeth the law, happy is he. Proverbs 29:18 (CEV)

The word vision used in this verse comes from the Hebrew root word "Chazah," which means "to gaze at, mentally to perceive or contemplate with pleasure". This vision can come by way of prophetic utterance, a dream, the written word of God or a rhema word from God.

My contextual definition for vision is "an internal or external revelation that deposits a picture in our hearts of a place, position, principle, promise or practice that's intended to keep us straight or turn us toward a purpose that is desired by God". Having a vision increases your expectation for the desired outcome by increasing your resolve to hold firm to the pathway that leads to the vision. It's like seeing something in front of you so clearly that you know if you just keep straight you can't miss it.

Revising Your Vision

This book of the law shall not depart out of thy mouth; but thou shalt meditate therein day and night, that thou mayest observe to do according to all that is written therein: for then thou shalt make thy way prosperous, and then thou shalt have good success.
Joshua 1:8

Initially, when I began to study the first eight verses of Joshua, I didn't understand why God had to repeatedly tell Joshua to be strong and courageous. My thoughts were that Joshua must have had a history like mine of falling short or giving up under life's pressures. After further research, I realized this was not the case. Joshua is first mentioned in Exodus 17:9 as an army commander that led the forces of Israel to victory over Amalek. Joshua goes on to lead the Israelite army in victory over thirty-one kings. So the question remains: Why did God need to repeatedly tell a war hero to be strong and courageous?

I began to realize that Joshua saw himself as Moses' right hand man, one able to take an order and follow it out to the finish; as long as Moses was telling Joshua what to do. He was able to stay in his comfort zone because the vision Joshua had of himself fit perfectly into what he was currently being required to do - which was follow the instructions of Moses.

Understanding this helped me to realize three personal, life-changing revelations. The first is that the current vision I have of myself will impede my ability to be strong and courageous in the next place God is preparing for me. The second is, as long as I continue to look at myself based on what I have already done, it will never properly prepare me for what God has yet bid me to do. Finally, just as God told Joshua He would be with him like He was with Moses; I should never look at myself based on my personal ability. I should look at myself based on God's ability working through me, in me and for me.

In essence God was telling Joshua and is telling us today, the key to getting ready for the next level assignment is not to focus on your personal limitations, but focus on God – the one who gives the assignment. We must always remember that God will never require us to do anything that he has not prepared us to do and is not willing to help us accomplish. So let's look at four practical keys to revising your vision.

See, Say, Do and Get

* <u>**See**</u> and meditate the vision

God wanted Joshua to meditate on the word until he had a clear picture in his mind of himself doing all that was written therein. This means we should literally meditate on the Word of God to the point that we actually see what God wanted Joshua to see; a vision of ourselves applying the supernatural Word of God to all of our natural situations. Remember, God told Joshua - and He is saying the same thing to us today through His Word - that we will make our own way prosperous and have good success in every area of life when we learn to live and apply the word of God. When you apply word based responses to your natural situations, it releases the supernatural power of God's Word into that situation to bring His Word to pass. This is how you generate prosperity and good success in your life by putting the weight of your challenges on God's Word and not on your back. Again, this process starts by meditating on the Word of God day and night until it's the only word that comes out of your mouth. Once you begin this process of daily meditating on the Word of God you should notice yourself gradually progressing through four stages of revelation.

The first is what I call **basic revelation**; this is when God starts revealing Himself to you at your level of comprehension. At this stage you will read scripture that you've read many times before but you will understand it differently, at a deeper level, as if God is giving you a personal explanation. Secondly, you should move to **internalized revelation**; this is revelation that has been personally and supernaturally deposited inside you. At this point it's no longer additional information that you carry in your head it has now become a life altering word that's deposited in your heart by way of significant pondering and careful consideration. Thirdly, you should move into **personal revelation**, this is when you realize that God is personally speaking to you through His Word. At this point you understand that the Word of God is not revealed to change the world around you, but to change you. The last stage is **synthesized revelation**. This is revelation that has become part of your decision making process by way of integration into your personal and permanent view of reality to the point of being something that is always considered when personal decisions are being made.

- **Say** faith-filled confessions

Let us hold fast the profession of our faith without wavering; (for he is faithful that promised;) Hebrews 10:23

The word 'confess' is the Greek word "homologeo," which means "to profess or acknowledge". This word comes from the base words - homo: which means "the same" and logeo: which means "word or something said". So in essence the word confess here means to agree with God, to say the same as God or to openly declare what God says in His Word about you. Simply put, a confession is when we repeat out loud what God has already said in His Word. Confessing the word regularly has many significant benefits such as helping you keep your focus in the right direction by focusing on the savior and not the situation. Confession also builds your faith. Romans 10:17 says *"So then faith cometh by hearing, and hearing by the word of God"*. This means hearing the Word of God is what builds your faith even when that word is coming out of your own mouth. Confession will also guard your heart, your mind and your peace. Isaiah 26:3 reminds us that *"Thou wilt keep him in perfect peace, whose mind is stayed on thee: because he trusteth in thee"*. In other words, a positive confession will drown out the negative impressions of the world and protect your heart and mind from receiving what goes against what you see and say in the word.

- **Do**; actions speak loudly too!

God told Joshua to meditate until he saw himself doing in his own life, what he witnessed in scripture. In other words, you are to start acting like you believe that what you see and what you say about yourself is true. Remember, demonstration is what validates declaration and it is your actions, lining up with your confession that gives life and legs to the faith process. In other words; it's your actions or the things you do that gives God something tangible to respond to; especially when your actions are your faith filled responses to the Word of God in your situation. There should always be a corresponding action to the words you have spoken, because faith without works is dead.

- **Get** is the return on your effort and your decision to apply the Word of God to your life.

Your actions that line up with scripture will produce predictable results in your life. If you say what you see and do what you say – you will get what you saw and said. scripture clearly tells us that we will most assuredly reap what we sow. So, when I see, say and do the Word of God, I will receive the manifestation or Gods intended outcome for that word validated in my life.

Ponder Point: If you start saying what you see and start doing what you say, you'll start getting what you're saying and what you're seeing.

Corresponding Confession: (to be spoken aloud)

When I begin to look at myself through the Word of God and see myself through the eyes of God, the question should never be, "Do I have what it takes to overcome my failures and overpower my challenges?"
God's word says that I am fully supplied, thoroughly

furnished and filled with the living Spirit of the Living God. I walk in the presence of God, displaying the character of God, inheriting the promises of God while demonstrating the power of God that lives inside of me. I am who God says I am and I can do what God said I can do. I now have a vision of who I really am and this vision will empower me to live free from my past and boldly embrace the new person I am in Christ.

Chapter Four:

How to Endure Temptation

*Blessed is the man that endureth temptation: for when
he is tried, he shall receive the crown of life, which
the Lord hath promised to them that love him.*
James 1:12

Once you know that God is in control and without limits, and
begin to realize your true identity and capabilities through your
relationship with God, you will become a threat and a target to the
forces of evil and experience an accelerated barrage of attacks.
These attacks from the enemy are geared to stop you from
exercising your authority and living the life of victory that God has
made available to every believer. These attacks generally come in
various forms of temptations that can distract, detour or literally
disconnect you from God and your destiny path. It is vitally
important at this point that you understand temptation and gather
the needed tools to endure it successfully.

In order to have a sound fundamental understanding of
temptation we should take a close look at the 1st chapter of James.
It's here that the Bible gives us clarity on the meaning, the origin
and the purpose temptation serves in the life of the believer. The
word 'temptation' used in the following verses comes from the
Greek word "peirasmos" and it means "an experiment, attempt, or
trial to test ones fidelity, integrity, virtue and constancy". The
Bible also infers it is "an attempt to entice one to sin, adversity,
affliction" or "trouble sent by God to test or prove one's character,
faith and holiness".

We need to be clear on the fact that these trials and tests can
come from God, the devil or our flesh. We know from the Bible

that temptations or tests that originate from satan are meant to kill, steal and destroy. His plan is to steal your faith in the power of the Word of God, kill your ability to live and function in a way that is pleasing to God, thus destroying your usefulness to God. On the contrary, God's tests are to reveal, build and display. They reveal the level of faith we have, build the level of faith we need so we can display the level of faith it takes to succeed in the things of God.

Let's look at James 1:2-4 and identify some critical observations about temptation.

V2: *"My brethren, count it all joy when ye fall into divers temptations."* The word 'fall' used in this verse is the Greek word "peripiptō", which means "to be surrounded with". This tells us that, no matter how godly we try to live, temptation will always be common and unavoidable in our lives. It also tells us that these trials and tests should not be viewed as something bad, but should be viewed as something good and essential for the development of the Christian in Christ-like character.

V3: *"Knowing this, that the trying of your faith worketh patience."* This verse explains why temptation is necessary and important in the life of the believer - temptation produces patience. This helps us to understand that the tests and trials are the actual ingredients or the recipe that God uses to produce patience. Therefore temptation - whether it comes from God, our flesh or the devil will always produce patience in the believer who endures the temptation. This is not a test to see if you have faith; it's a test to see if you're willing to apply the measure of faith you already have. As we read in 1Corinthians 10:13, God will not allow us to be tempted above our present ability to withstand the temptation. This means God will not allow us to take a test that we aren't equipped to pass. The passing of a test or the enduring of a trial is never predicated on the situation, it's based on our personal decision to serve God and not ourselves.

V4: *"But let patience have [her] perfect work, that ye may be perfect and entire, wanting nothing."* This verse shows us that patience is the critical tool God uses in the shaping and development of our character. To put this in perspective we should understand that patience itself is not the destination, it's the vehicle that God uses to get you through the process, to learn what you need to learn, to function at the destination God is preparing you for. We will never be able to learn what God needs to teach us or grow into the people that God needs us to be, if we're not willing and able to stay in the process. We must understand, it is a developmental opportunity that God is using to get us ready. And that means we must develop patience.

Scripture is pretty clear that temptation is the tool God uses to build patience. The dictionary definition of patience is: "an ability or willingness to suppress restlessness or annoyance when confronted with delay". The Greek word is "hupomone" which means "cheerful or hopeful steadfastness, constancy, and endurance". My contextual definition is simply "the ability to wait with the right attitude". In essence, patience enables us to go through what we need to go through, to get where we need to get to, while maintaining the proper attitude throughout the developmental process.

Ponder Point: No matter how godly we try to live, we will never be able to avoid temptation so we will have to learn how to endure it.

Before we move on in our study on temptation I want to point out two key facts about patience. First: Patience is a Godly attribute. Rom. 15:5 says *"Now the God of patience and of comfort grant you to be of the same mind one with another according to Christ Jesus."* So we can see in scripture as well as in our own lives that God is patient.

Secondly: Patience is necessary for receiving the promises of God. Heb. 6:2 urges *"That ye be not slothful, but followers of them who through faith and patience inherit the promises."* We see additional text on this in Hebrews 10:36 which reads, *"For ye have need of patience, that, having done the will of God, ye may receive the promise"*. So, we need faith to do God's will but we must add patience to our faith to receive God's promise. Faith gives you the ability to step out on the Word of God, but patience gives you the ability to hold on to that word until it comes to pass in your life.

Let's continue our study on temptation in the book of James by focusing on verses 12 through 15.

V.12: *Blessed is the man that endureth temptation: for when he is tried, he shall receive the crown of life, which the Lord hath promised to them that love him.* This verse tells us that God blesses (makes happy) the man that endureth and remains faithful during times of temptation. It also tells us we can actually be tempted and still not sin because temptation and sin are not the same. So being tempted, in and of itself, is not sin. It is only when we yield to that temptation that sin actually occurs. An example of this: you see someone drop twenty dollars, you pick it up and are tempted to keep it, but you decide to give it back. At the point you were actually considering keeping the money you were in temptation. However, that temptation did not cross over into sin because you did not yield to the temptation; you endured unto righteousness by returning the money.

V.13: *Let no man say when he is tempted, I am tempted of God: for God cannot be tempted with evil, neither tempteth he any man:* God will never entice us to do anything that is contrary to His Word. God will, however, test us to see if we will hold on to His Word under adverse circumstances. We see in Genesis 22:1-11 that God did tempt (test) Abraham's faith when He told Abraham to sacrifice his son Isaac as a burnt offering. We can also see in this encounter that God never intended for Isaac to die but for Abraham to live through and depend on his faith in God.

V.14: *But every man is tempted, when he is drawn away of his own lust, and enticed.* This tells us that the origin of temptation is internal, never external, meaning the devil can dangle something in front of you all day long but if you don't have a desire or a propensity that draws you to it you will not be tempted. Think about it, if I held a worm in front of you and told you how good it tastes and how healthy it is for your body, would you eat the worm? My point is, you're not going to be tempted by things you don't like, so when you find yourself tempted you need to assume responsibility for the temptation. Then you must put safeguards or barriers in place to protect yourself as you begin the process of strengthening yourself in that area.

I remember a few years ago when I taught this lesson, one of the students came up after class and said he had to stop reading the newspaper because he was having problems handling the lingerie section. Another student said he was blaming the newspaper for his issues. I stepped in at that point and said he was not blaming it on the newspaper. On the contrary, he had taken ownership of his inability to handle the lingerie section properly; so by not buying the paper he was putting safeguards and barriers in place to protect himself until he had more strength in that area. He was willing to do what it took to keep from sinning. Which, by the way, is not a sign of weakness it's a sign of strength, wisdom and a desire to be pleasing to God

V.15: *Then when lust hath conceived, it bringeth forth sin: and sin, when it is finished, bringeth forth death.* As we read in earlier verses the reward of enduring temptation is patience and blessings. But we see in this verse that sinful desires that are not aborted will always birth sin (the desire acted out) and sin that's not apprehended and repented for, will ultimately cause death. This could be physical death or death in the sense that you become of no use or dead to the things of God by disqualifying yourself from the opportunity of accomplishing what God created you to do.

Ponder Point: When you find yourself tempted or in temptation, make sure you understand the external environment, but realize it's the internal pull of what's inside of you that's causing you to be tempted.

Now that we have a fundamental understanding of temptation, let's examine the progression of temptation as it relates to the devil and our flesh. Let's take a look at what I call Six Steps in the Tempters Methodology as seen in Luke 4:1-13. These steps are important to take notice of because 2Corinthians 2:11 tells us we can keep satan from getting an advantage over us by becoming aware of how he operates.

Six Steps in the Tempters Methodology

1. Watching and waiting: (Luke 4:1-3)

And Jesus being full of the Holy Ghost returned from Jordan, and was led by the Spirit into the wilderness, [2]Being forty days tempted of the devil. And in those days he did eat nothing: and when they were ended, he afterward hungered. [3]And the devil said unto him, If thou be the Son of God, command this stone that it be made bread.

We can clearly see that the devil was waiting on an opportunity to catch Jesus in what he presumed to be a vulnerable state. We read in 1Peter 5:8 that we are to *"Be sensible and vigilant, because your adversary the Devil walks about like a roaring lion, seeking someone he may devour"*. Some time ago I watched a program on National Geographic about lions and how they hunt. Lions normally don't go after the strongest prey or those that congregate in groups. They go after the weakest, the youngest, the sickest or those who have lost focus and gotten separated from the pack. The devil, like a roaring lion, is always waiting on us to get too tired, too sad, too happy, too broke, too rich or any condition that causes us to put our guards down and separate ourselves from the pack. He is looking for the weak, wounded and wandering, in essence, the 'devourables'. The weak are those who don't build themselves up daily through the Word, prayer and interactions with other believers. The wounded are those who refuse to forgive themselves and others and still hold on to the shame, guilt, anger and pain received from others and their own past mistakes. The wandering are those who have strayed away from the principles, practices and disciplines that have kept them safe in the past; thus rendering themselves unprotected and vulnerable to attack.

2. Attacks the mind or thinking process:

The first word used in the attack on Jesus was "if". This was the devils attempt to create doubt and confusion in the mind of Christ. Since the mind is the place where we receive and process information and then determine what action needs to be taken, it becomes the logical place to launch an attack. What we think will always precede what we do in any given situation. The devil understands that doubt cancels faith and confusion cancels your ability to respond quickly and correctly to the attack. The devil knows your ability to resist and defeat him is rooted in an unwavering faith in God, His Word, His grace and the authority He has given you as a believer and child of God.

3. Seeks to exploit pride: (Luke 4:3,9)

And the devil said unto him, If thou be the Son of God, command this stone that it be made bread...⁹ And he brought him to Jerusalem, and set him on a pinnacle of the temple, and said unto him, If thou be the Son of God, cast thyself down from hence:

The devil understands the consequences of pride, as well as the fact that we are all prone to indulge in it if we are not careful. Pride caused satan to reject the position God had given him because his pride told him he should be God's equal. Satan in turn used the same tactic on Eve in the garden when he told her if she ate the apple she would be like God. Even though she was created in God's image and likeness and given reign over the earth, pride caused her to believe she should be an equal with God. It is a human characteristic to want to be recognized, to rise to the top of our field or be given credit for something we have done. This in and of itself is fine, as long as you don't take credit for what God enabled, empowered or allowed you to accomplish. The Bible tells us to be clothed in humility because God resists the proud. If the devil can get you into pride, it makes it easier for him to keep you in bondage because pride separates us from our real source of strength. Pride tells us we are all the strength we need.

4. Offers you a portion of what you already have: (Luke 4:5-7)

And the devil, taking him up into an high mountain, shewed unto him all the kingdoms of the world in a moment of time ⁶ And the devil said unto him, All this power will I give thee, and the glory of them: for that is delivered unto me; and to whomsoever I will I give it. ⁷ If thou therefore wilt worship me, all shall be thine.

We see that the devil offered Jesus power over the kingdoms of the world. This may sound like a lot to somebody who doesn't know better, but Romans 8:17 tells us that the earth, the heavens and the fullness thereof already belong to God, to Jesus and to us. We are God's children and joint-heirs with Christ. This would be the equivalent of offering someone a piece of their own pie. In essence, the devil couldn't offer Jesus anything. He was actually trying to get Jesus to forfeit what He already owned by turning away from God and disconnecting Himself from His promised inheritance.

It is really important that you lock this in your mind. The things satan tries to give you are geared to produce short-term satisfaction and rob you of long-term fulfillment of purpose. Remember Eve? The apple was pleasing to the eye and the pallet (short term satisfaction) but she lost the opportunity to fulfill her purpose. She forfeited the chance to experience God's power working in her life and the personal relationship she previously shared with God. Think about it, the only things the devil can own are things that are not already owned by God. That would be lies, confusion, and the lives of those who have rejected or have yet to accept Jesus as Lord and Savior. The devil knows how to make sin sound good, look good and fit into pretty packages. Once again let's remember Eve so we don't settle for a piece of the pie when we can have the whole promise.

5. <u>Intends to render you useless to God: (Luke 4:10)</u>

We see in Luke 4:10 that the devil is quoting scripture although he did not quote it correctly, the point is he knows the Bible. The devil knew Jesus was the Son of God and the only chance for reconciliation between God and man. The devil also knew that man could not serve two masters. So, if Jesus would receive the devil as Lord through an act of worship, it would minimize His ability to serve God. Therefore, Jesus would be rendered useless to God and the purpose that God sent Him to fulfill.

6. <u>Backs off to plan for the next attack: (Luke 4:12)</u>

And Jesus answering said unto him, It is said, Thou shalt not tempt the Lord thy God.

Luke 4:12 tells us that the devil departed for a season. This makes it very clear that he will go back to step one, watching and waiting for the next opportunity to launch his next attack. James 4:7 says, *"submit yourselves therefore to God resist the devil and he will flee"*. Just remember, the fleeing is temporary, so the resisting must continue.

Just as it is important to understand the devices of satan and how he attacks, it is also important to understand the devices of the flesh. Remember the Bible says we are tempted when we are drawn away by our own lust and lust resides in our flesh. So let's look at six keys to understanding the progression of temptation through its attacks on the flesh.

Six Keys to Understanding the Progression of Temptation Through the Lust of the Flesh. Attacks:

1) Start in the mind, your thought life:

Our flesh is always transmitting thoughts to our minds, but we must be very careful how we respond to those thoughts. Scripture tells us in Romans 7:18 that no good thing dwells in our flesh and John 6:63 tells us that our flesh profits nothing. This means that our flesh will never be a willing participant in our spiritual endeavors, it will only seek to satisfy itself. This is why you can stay up all night watching television or dancing at a nightclub and not feel tired. Yet as soon as you decide to stay home, cut off the TV and study your Bible, it seems that by 9:00 p.m. you can't keep your eyes open. Then, if somebody calls and invites you out - you wake right up.

2) Increases intensity and frequency:

When our flesh sends the message to our mind that it wants a drink, a drug, a smoke or any other source of satisfaction, we must be prepared for these thoughts to increase in intensity and frequency. Our flesh will act like a baby that wants to be picked up, the child will cry louder and harder trying to get you to give what it perceives will make it feel better.

3) <u>Seeks to overwhelm the senses:</u>

Our flesh has a tendency to try to overwhelm or overpower the senses to make you feel that things are worse than they are, to get you to respond in a way that will satisfy its lustful appetites. In Genesis 25 we see a good example of this being played out in the lives of Esau and his younger brother Jacob. Esau, being the first-born son of Isaac, was entitled to the first-born birthright, but sold that birthright to his brother Jacob for a bowl of soup because he was hungry. The two points I want to make are these: first; your flesh will try to overwhelm your better judgment to convince you to settle for instant gratification and give no consideration to the long-term effects. This is why people buy things they really want, but don't really need, knowing they can't really afford it. Secondly, your flesh has no real regard for you or others and will always try to manipulate your mind to please its own lust.

4) <u>Seeks to make you anxious:</u>

When we get anxious, nervous or antsy and feel that we need to do something right now and can't wait, this is the flesh. Your flesh doesn't want you to pray and wait for an answer, it just wants you to listen to it and respond. This reminds me of a sales person who tries to get you all hyped up, then tells you if you don't make an immediate decision you will lose the deal. This is because they know if they give you time to settle down and think, it will become easier for you to walk away. Remember, anxiousness or anxiety is the opposite of patience. Where patience gives you the ability to wait on God; anxiousness will become your god by dictating your attitude and actions.

5) <u>Makes you feel sin is inevitable:</u>

Once you reach a certain point of anxiety, you can begin to feel like you must follow through on those thoughts. I have been there on many occasions and have talked to many others who have also experienced this. It is during these times that you feel you are no longer in control and your flesh has taken over. Although in the next section I'm going to talk about how to handle temptation, I want to mention here that your flesh, or the devil, can't actually take control. They can only try to make you think and feel that way in order to get you to circumvent your authority.

6) <u>Seeks to cause a temporary dulling of the spiritual senses:</u>

When the flesh is bombarding you with self-gratifying thoughts, it can temporarily dull your spiritual senses. This is one of the reasons regular fasting is important in helping you hear God more clearly. It is not because fasting makes God talk louder; it just makes it easier to hear Him when we quiet the distractions of the flesh.

Enduring and Overcoming Temptation

In this section I want to discuss some practical keys that I believe will set you up for success in enduring the inevitable; temptation.

In order to get ready for something, the preparation must begin before the actual encounter. So now that you know temptation is inevitable it would be foolish for you not to prepare an adequate strategy for success. Successful Christian living is the outward manifestation of a predetermined set of biblical disciplines and principles that govern our thinking and actions. In order for this to happen, these disciplines and principles must be practiced with such diligence that they are no longer just what you do, but ultimately determine the person you become. When this happens you will have effectively synthesized these disciplines and principles into your internal decision-making process to the degree they will become the foundation for all your outward actions and responses. Romans 12:1-3 calls this renewing your mind and thus transforming your ability to respond to God's will for your life. Now let me give you three focus points that will help you stay ready for the temptation we must all face.

- Stay prayed up

We learned in Chapter 1 that God is the source of our strength and that source is accessed through prayer. It's vitally important that we start each day in communion with God through prayer. And that we open ourselves to Him, thus willingly opening a path for Him to share Himself with us. This is the time where we affirm our dedication while seeking direction for the day ahead. David fully understood that God is omniscient and knows what test, trials and temptations the day will bring. In Psalms 143:8 David prays, *"Let the morning bring me word of your unfailing love, for I have put my trust in you. Show me the way I should go, for I lift up my soul."* Prayer is probably the greatest power on earth, for prayer moves the hand that moves the world and puts you in position for that same hand to move you. Start each day with a conversation with God, asking Him for wisdom, direction and His plan for your day.

- Stay worded up

In Luke Chapter 4, the devil knew Jesus would be weak considering he had not eaten in 40 days. There in V.4 after the first temptation, Jesus makes a powerful statement that sets the tone for this entire encounter, as well as every demonic encounter that we will ever face. Jesus says, *"It is written, that man shall not live by bread alone, but by every word from the mouth of God"*. This tells us that although man might exhibit a weakness, as long as he continues to nourish himself with the Word of God it will give him overall strength to resist the area of weakness and maintain stability in keeping God's will for his life until the area of weakness has been properly nourished back to strength.

- Stay on guard

Watch and pray, that ye enter not into temptation: the spirit indeed is willing, but the flesh is weak. Matt 26:41

When you properly post a guard, you need to tell the guard what it is that they need to watch for. They need to be familiar with the ways and means the enemy has used in the past, and also know the strengths and weaknesses of what they are guarding. So, here's the deal, you have to take ownership of guarding yourself. To effectively do this you need to take some time and write down your strengths and weaknesses and make a note of every situation and method the devil and your flesh has used successfully to tempt you to sin in the past. Again, if you are going to be a good guard, you need to know what to look for and then have a plan in place to properly handle and overcome the expected attacks or temptations. This will help you notice attacks/temptations sooner and respond quicker and more efficiently which leads me to the next point about interrupters and pre-planned responses.

- Interrupters and Pre-planned responses

Guard your heart above all else, for it determines the course of your life. Proverbs 4:23 (NLT)

Proverbs 4 reinforces the fact that the attack starts in the mind and therefore our minds should be guarded at all times, at all cost. The scripture actually implies that your thought life, or the things you think about, will ultimately determine the course or the direction that your life will take. So if you were to look at where you currently are in your life - the good, the bad and the ugly - it can all be traced back to the things you spent your time thinking about leading up to where you are now. In other words, when you learn how to control your thinking, you also learn how to control your direction. Simply put, changing your thinking will change your life.

Will you be consistently overcome by the temptations of this life or will you be a consistent overcomer? In 3rd John 2 (MKJV) we read *"Beloved, in regard to all things I pray that you prosper and be in health, even as your soul prospers"*. The word 'soul' used in this verse is the Greek word "psuchē" that often translates as the word "mind". The word 'prospers' used in that verse is the Greek word "euodoō" that means "to help on the road" or "succeed in reaching". So we could say, the help we need on the road of life to reach God's predestined purpose is based on the prospering of our minds. Therefore it is vitally important that you first monitor each thought. Second, determine if it's a healthy thought that leads you in the way of godliness, or if it is an unhealthy thought that needs to be immediately discarded.

The sooner you can identify an ungodly thought, the quicker

you get rid of it and the better off you will be. The Bible tells us that as a man thinketh in his heart so is he. The thoughts that start in your head that you don't deal with will eventually seat themselves in your heart. The Bible says once this happens you will act out accordingly, regardless if the thought is good or bad. This explains why people who have spent most of their lives doing kind and gentle things for others, find themselves in serious trouble and struggle to figure out how they lost their self-control. This is most likely because their negative thoughts that weren't dealt with, inevitably turned into the negative outburst of actions. Again the Bible is clear if you don't catch a bad thought at head level and allow it to get to heart level, chances are you will respond according to the thought.

Every time I conduct a biblical counseling session with someone who has done something they thought they would never do, or with someone who had stopped a certain behavior and then picked it up again, I always ask them when the thoughts started. The answers are always the same - the thoughts started well before the action, became more frequent, and got stronger and harder to resist. A major key in predicting and preventing future behavior is how you handle ungodly thoughts when they arise.

Now let me share with you the two-part strategy God gave me years ago that I use and have been teaching others to use with great success. The first part is simply called interrupters. The sole purpose of the interrupter is to interrupt or disrupt the negative thought as soon as possible. I know you may be thinking this sounds too easy, well, praise God, it is easy but more importantly - praise God it works.

Five or six years ago I was looking at television with the remote in my hand and it was as if the Lord asked me what should you do when you don't want to watch the program that's on. Naturally my answer was change the channel. The act of changing the channel does two things. It interrupts the current program you are watching and then it takes you to a new program. So the first thing I do when I get a thought that I don't want to continue is to tell myself to change the channel. Again this interrupts the flow of the current thought and allows me to redirect my thinking. In teaching this over the years people have come up with many different interrupters. Some, like me, use phrases, others use scriptures, still others use the names of their children or the names of people who are important to them. The interrupter you use is your choice, but it must be practiced and there must be a commitment to use it every time you get a thought that could tempt you to sin or detour you from divine destiny. Remember, you don't have control over the thoughts that drop into your head, but you do have control over which ones are allowed to stay.

The second part of this process is pre-planned responses. Once a thought has been interrupted, you need a predetermined place to direct your thinking. Without a pre-planned response, you take the risk of going from one bad thought to another. That will definitely weaken your ability to immediately get your thoughts back on the prosperity road to success. My personal pre-planned response is to start praising God. Again, once I interrupt the bad thought, I replace it with a thought of praising God. I just start praising God for everything I can think of, and I do it until I feel that the negative thought has been completely cast down.

Although I encourage people to use whatever interrupter they like, I strongly suggest - until God tells you differently - use praise as your pre-planned response. Psalms 22:3 says *"But thou art holy, O thou that inhabitest the praises of Israel"*. The word 'inhabitest' means "to dwell, abide, sit down and make, to keep". So when you are praising God, the very presence of God and power of God literally sits down and dwells in the midst of your praise. Then Psalms 22:4 says *"Our fathers trusted in thee: they trusted, and thou didst deliver them"*. It's never a question whether or not God can deliver us; the question is whether or not we will put ourselves in position for His power to be present when we need it. Praise will make that happen.

I will admit, there are days in my life when it seems that every five minutes the devil, or my flesh, is attacking my mind. I never change my responses because I know if my actions are repeatable then so are my outcomes. I won last time and I'll win next time, because I have identified and implemented a strategy that works. Sometimes when the attacks are coming fast and furious, I add insult to injury by telling the devil that he will get tired of attacking me, before I get tired of praising my God. Following are some additional strategies to help fortify your endurance in this matter:

1. Remember it is a spiritual fight not a physical fight

Take some time here and read 2Corinthians 10:3-5 and Ephesians 6:10-19. These scriptures tell us that our fight to endure temptation is not a physical fight it's a spiritual fight so we must put on our spiritual battle gear if we expect to win. We do this by intentionally arming ourselves with the six pieces of armor described in Ephesians 6:10-19.

- Having your loins girt about with truth:

This is the belief that every word of God is true. This truth becomes the foundation for your attitude, actions and advances against the enemy and keeps you from failing in the midst of temptations, tests and trials. Our ability to function as true believers is predicated on three foundational truths. The Word of God is true. God is who He says He is, He can do what He says He can do, we are who God said we are and we can do what God said we can do. These truths become the belt that the other armour is attached to and activated by.

- Breastplate of righteousness:

This is having a holy character or moral conduct that governs your way of life and the way you interact with others. Have you ever met someone who is consistently soft spoken, always tries to do the right thing, never uses profanity and never raises their voice? What would be your first thought if someone came to you and told you that person screamed and cursed them out. You would most likely have a hard time accepting that because it contradicts the character they have consistently displayed. Having on the breastplate of righteousness becomes evident when your actions and your Godly beliefs line up to produce Godly character. It sets itself in front of you to validate your witness by protecting you against attempted character assassination. When your actions consistently line up with the Word, your established character will combat any lies launched against you with the intent to assassinate your character and bring disrepute to the Kingdom.

- Feet Shod with the Preparation of the gospel of peace:

This is when your feet have been properly protected, prepared for the battle and readied to proclaim the gospel of peace. This produces a level of boldness that allows you to take the fight to the enemy and also keeps you from getting frustrated and losing your peace during times of perceived stagnation.

- The shield of faith or the shield which is faith:

The shield of faith is a large shield that is placed between you and the enemy to facilitate full body protection. The fiery darts launched by the enemy will hit your faith/shield and not you. It must be noted, that after the fiery darts are stopped by this shield, they are also extinguished. In other words, they are not allowed to create other problems or distractions in other areas of your life. If you have ever watched an old cowboy and Indian movie you would have noticed when the Indians were fighting the cowboys they would dip their arrows in flammable liquid before they launched them. The reasoning was if the arrow itself wasn't a direct hit or was blocked by a protective shield, it would still cause other problems that would distract them from the fight. You see, if you're focusing on the fire, you're not focusing on the fight. That meant the cowboys had to put down their weapons and come from behind their shields to extinguish the flames the fiery darts started. Thank God He has not only given us a shield that will protect us from a direct hit, but also protects from residual damage meant to distract us and make us come from behind our shields.

- The helmet of salvation.

The helmet of salvation keeps your mind and thoughts covered with the assurance of your salvation. This keeps you from ever doubting God's love, your relationship, your son-ship, your heritage or the power that's been promised to you by God.

- The sword of the Spirit, which is the Word of God.

The Greek term used for 'word' is "rhēma" which means – "thing spoken, what one has said, a declaration of one's mind made in words or an utterance". This is important because it means you use the word of God by declaring it. In others words, you swing and cut with the sword/word of the spirit by verbally declaring it at your situation/temptation. Remember in Luke 4, Jesus didn't just remember the Word, He used it as His weapon on His enemy.

- Praying always.

We should strive for our communion with God to become a life style in which we seek continued direction from God for every task and challenge in every area of our lives.

2. <u>Front load your faith</u>

Most believers who have struggled with any kind of addiction or bondage don't know how to keep score properly. I would go for days and sometimes months before falling back again, but as soon as I messed up, the first thing out of my mouth was "I just can't stay sober, I'm always messing up and I just don't know what to do". A few years ago while listening to another believer say almost the same thing, the Holy Spirit revealed to me that he had not learned how to properly keep score. I told him "Brother you don't know how to keep score". Now you know he probably thought just what you're thinking right know, that I must be crazy. So you probably can't keep score either! Just joking, but let me explain.

In this particular case he was dealing with a pornography issue, he would go for months at a time before he indulged. I asked him how often he was tempted. He said the thoughts normally come at least once a day, usually more. I told him if the thoughts came only once a day and he had gone three months without indulging, the actual score was 90 to 1 in his favor. In essence, he already had a testimony and a strategy for success, but the devil duped him into only keeping score in the loss column. He never added up his victories. The devil knew if all he could see was what he did wrong, one day he would not be able to lock in on his successes and repeat what he had done right the other ninety days.

Psalms 78:9-11 says, *"The sons of Ephraim were archers equipped with bows, Yet they turned back in the day of battle. [10]They did not keep the covenant of God And refused to walk in His law;* [11]*They forgot His deeds And His miracles that He had shown them".*

This scripture tells us that even when God has equipped us with the tools and a strategy for success, the strength to continue comes from remembering and rehearsing the testimonies of what God has done. Remember, we overcome by the blood of the lamb and the words of our testimony. Sure, you should identify what you did wrong, but you should focus on repeating what you did right. Carefully look back over your life, analyze the victories and see what they have in common. This will strengthen you moving forward and serve as a reminder that if your actions are repeatable, so are your outcomes. If one of the definitions of insanity is doing the same thing and expecting different results, then we could say sanity is doing the same thing and expecting the same results.

1Corinthians 15:57 tells us that we should be thankful to God who has given us the victory through our Lord Jesus Christ. This means victory is always an option if we are willing to live by the Word of God. If God says He has given me the victory, then the victory is mine. Now the key here is expectation. Remember I said in Chapter 2 that your expectation determines your effort and your effort determines your outcome. If you don't really believe you have the victory, you will never be able to overcome the perceived obstacles. You will not be able to produce the level of faith, effort and consistent focus necessary to manifest the victory in every area of your life.

3. Remember, you always have a choice

As we have already discussed 1Corinthians 10:13 is a powerful and empowering scripture if you don't read it like poetry, but read it as a biblical principle that will always be enforced by God. This does not say we will not be tempted, it says we will not be tempted above our ability to resist. In other words, God will not let you be confronted by a situation that He has not already prepared and empowered you to win the victory over.

Now I've got to make a very strong statement that's true to every believer whether you are familiar with this principle or not. Every time you are tempted and yield to that temptation - and sin -

it is because you chose sin over salvation. Believe me, I did not want to say it like that, but that's the way you need to hear it. You must understand that neither your flesh nor the devil can overwhelm you and force you to commit sin. Contrary to comedian Flip Wilson, the devil can't make you do it! If that were the case it would mean that God provides inadequate protection and we know that's not true, so you have to look at yourself and the choice you made.

Once you understand this principle you also understand that you don't have to lose to temptation in the future; if you don't want to. God will always give you the strength to make the right choice but He will never override your right to choose for yourself. The word escape doesn't mean you don't have to go through the temptation. It means God will always make sure you have a way through the temptation and a landing place, a place to land intact on the other side of the test.

You may be wondering, "What do I do if I fall to temptation?" The answer is simple - don't stay down. Scripture tells us in Proverbs 24:16, that a just man falls seven times, and rises up again: but the wicked shall fall into mischief. This is not to say you will fall or that it's alright to fall, but to teach you how to get up if you do fall. Think about this, if you fall, the fall is no longer the most important thing. What's most important at that point is what you do next. So here is the three step process I use and teach after a fall occurs.

How to Handle a Fall

1) Confess, repent, ask for forgiveness and move on

If we confess our sins, he is faithful and just to forgive us our sins, and to cleanse us from all unrighteousness 1John 1:9

Confess here simply means to understand and agree that we have sinned. When we agree with God that we have sinned, repent or make a decision not to continue in that sin and ask God to forgive us, He will forgive our sin. But the scripture indicates that God doesn't just stop there. It goes on to say that God cleanses us from all unrighteousness. This means that after God forgives us He will remove the stain, shame and guilt that sin has left on our soul (heart or inner man). Do you remember when you were young and were told to stay clean? So you tried to play in the dirt without getting dirty; and your mom found you all filthy. She took you in the house, got you all cleaned up, then put clean clothes on you. My point is this, once you had been washed clean and put on the clean clothes; there was no evidence of the filth you were in just a short time ago. Move on.

2) Remember, God doesn't condemn

When Jesus had lifted up himself, and saw none but the woman, he said unto her, Woman, where are those thine accusers? Hath no man condemned thee? She said, No man, Lord. And Jesus said unto her, neither do I condemn thee: go, and sin no more.
John 8:10-11

Where is the god who can compare with you— wiping the slate clean of guilt, Turning a blind eye, a deaf ear, to the past sins of your purged and precious people? You don't nurse your anger and don't stay angry long, for mercy is your specialty. That's what you love most. And compassion is on its way to us. You'll stamp out our wrongdoing. You'll sink our sins to the bottom of the ocean. You'll stay true to your word to Father Jacob and continue the compassion you showed Grandfather Abraham—Everything you promised our ancestors from a long time ago.
Micah 7:18-20 (MSG)

Many people are walking around still holding on to sin they have already been forgiven of and having a very difficult time reaching out to God because they feel God is still angry about a sin they have already repented of. The Bible tells us that after God forgives our sin, he puts our sins out of His sight and when He looks at us he doesn't see our sin; just our righteousness through Christ. We don't have to feel guilty going to God because He won't keep bringing up our past mistakes. He has actually forgotten them. Remember, God is not concerned about where we've been He is concerned about where we're going.

3) <u>Tell someone, (don't keep it a secret) and engage the power of agreement</u>

Two are better than one; because they have a good reward for their labour. [10] For if they fall, the one will lift up his fellow: but woe to him that is alone when he falleth; for he hath not another to help him up. Ecclesiastics 4:9-10

Confess your faults one to another, and pray one for another, that ye may be healed. The effectual fervent prayer of a righteous man availeth much. James 5:16

The longer you hide a sin the longer that sin will have a hold on you. The quicker you tell somebody when you fall, the quicker you can get the help you need to get up. I do understand there is some shame incurred when we fall, but it's not nearly as much shame as staying down when help is available. A wise man once said character is not defined in the fall it's defined in your response to the fall. Although scripture is clear that temptation is inevitable it can be minimized when proper precautions are taken and walls of protection are built.

3 Key Strategies to Building Walls

A man without self-control is like a city broken into and left without walls. Proverb 25:28 (CEV)

In the Bible we see walls around cities, temples, houses and vineyards. In essence we see walls around anything you want to keep separate or protected. So, walls were designed for separation, protection and a defense shield.

1. <u>Decide what you just don't do and were you just won't go</u>

Plan carefully what you do, and whatever you do will turn out right. [27]Avoid evil and walk straight ahead. Don't go one step off the right way. Proverb 4:26-27 (GNB)

I had to sit down and look at my life based on what I have

experienced, and the positive or negative results these experiences have produced. I then had to make some decisions on what things I should continue and what things I needed to stop altogether. It became clear that certain people and certain environments made it easy for me to exhibit past behaviors I was trying to keep in the past. I also noticed that certain environments and certain people inspired me to a higher level of godliness. I had to tell myself - if I am really serious about trying to live right, then I had to decide what I should discontinue doing and the places I should discontinue going. This simple exercise helped me to realize I must have a reason for everything I do. In other words, I no longer can afford to do things haphazardly, I actually have a reason that lines up with what I see and say in scripture. If you don't have a good reason for doing something let that be your good reason not to do it. If you follow this simple principle you're less likely to do something you'll regret later and more likely to be involved in things that please God, bless you and builds the Kingdom.

2. <u>Expose traps, triggers, and thoughts that got you in trouble before</u>

Now I know the Bible says a righteous man falls seven times, but it's not talking about falling in the same hole. I understand we are going to make mistakes but it's not alright to continue to make the same mistakes. To keep this from happening you must identify the traps, triggers, and thoughts that got you in trouble before; then set up barriers and roadblocks to protect yourself from repeating the behaviors.

Traps are situations you get yourself into by telling yourself, "this time the outcome will be different". For instance, you have a gambling problem and you go to the casino by yourself for dinner with no intentions of gambling, but four of the last five times you went, you ended up gambling. This is a trap.

Triggers are generally things you hear or see that set off flashbacks of things you have done in the past. They can be good or bad, but in the context of the lesson we're talking about, they are negative triggers. These can be names, movies, songs etc. If you're the person with that gambling problem you might not want to watch The World Series of Poker on TV. These triggers are different from traps because they don't put you in the actual environment. They put the virtual environment in your mind and as we learned earlier, this is where the attacks begin.

Because the attacks start in the mind there are some thoughts that you know you have no business holding on to. Such thoughts will eventually manifest themselves in your behavior. To keep this simple, if it's not a thought that holds you to the commitment you've made to walk upright; or a thought that lines up with scripture - just change the channel.

Scripture tells us if we want to be free from the worries of the world and have the peace of God in our lives we should only think about things that are true, noble, right, pure, lovely and honorable. If you train yourself to follow this model it will lead you to successful Christian living.

3. Decide new ways to handle old problems

But that isn't what you were taught about Jesus Christ. He is the truth, and you heard about him and learned about him. [22] You were told that your foolish desires will destroy you and that you must give up your old way of life with all its bad habits. [23] Let the Spirit change your way of thinking. Ephesians 4:21-23 (CEV)

Every situation in your life is not going to change just because you change. Remember you're the one that has changed, not the world around you. So even though they may not treat you differently, you still have to treat them differently. I remember when my boss wanted me to tell a lie because he thought it would make the workers feel better about what we had asked them to do. I had to explain to him that although he was my direct supervisor, God was my boss. That meant my work performance was not predicated on what was acceptable to him, but on what was acceptable to God; and lying was not acceptable. This may not have changed my boss, but it completely changed how he dealt with me and the level of respect and trust that he eventually developed for me. Our old way of doing things was predicated solely on addressing the situation at hand. Our new way of doing things is predicated on producing a desired outcome in line with God's will for our life. Example: if somebody says something to you that's completely out of order, the way of the world would be to check them hard and remind them who they are talking to. The new way, or the Word way of doing things says the desired outcome should determine our response. If peace and a display of godly character is the outcome you desire, then the response must be based on a godly characteristic or biblical principle. Case in point, the Bible says a soft word turns away wrath. So a soft word would be a proper response to produce the desired outcome. This means the new criteria for handling the old problem is responding to the world with the Word of God. This is something we will cover in depth in Chapter Five *Renewing the Mind.*

Enduring temptation is critical to developing godly character, attaining freedom from past and current strongholds and a having lifestyle that God can bless. Remember, James 1:12 says *"Blessed is the man that endureth temptation: for when he is tried, he shall receive the crown of life, which the Lord hath promised to them that love him."*

Chapter Five:

Forgiveness

*Then came Peter to him, and said, Lord, how oft shall
my brother sin against me, and I forgive him? till
seven times?* [22]*Jesus saith unto him, I say not unto
thee, Until seven times: but, Until seventy times seven*
Matthew 18:21-22

As we discussed in the last chapter, it is important to properly handle and endure temptation. I believe the temptation to hold on to an offense is one of the greatest and most frequent temptations we face as believers. I frequently hear terms like 'option' and 'process' as it relates to forgiveness, meaning its ok to forgive or not to forgive. If it takes a long time to forgive, it's alright because, after all - forgiveness is a process. These kinds of common, yet un-true, views about forgiveness make it one of the most successful strategies that satan uses to create confusion, separation and stagnation in the body of Christ. Many believers still feel the pain of some past event and find themselves unable to move forward and they can't figure out why. It's because unforgiveness is a stronghold that will lock on to your past pain, causing it to be more real and important than what God is currently trying to do in your life. It becomes hard to appreciate what's in front of you if you keep looking at what's behind you. You must either let go of what's in the past, in order to move forward, or hold on to the past and stay stuck right where you are. When Peter asked Jesus how many times should I forgive my brother when he sins against me, Jesus' answer made it clear that forgiveness is not a random action. It is the standard for forward motion in the life of a believer. The word 'forgive' used in Matthew 18 is the Greek word "aphiemi" which means "to lay aside, leave, let alone or put away". We can see here that the focus is not on what was done to you but on how you should respond to it. In essence, forgiveness means to give up or lay aside all resentment or claim to requital on an account, an offense or to pardon or cancel a debt. This means you recognized and acknowledge what was done to you or taken from you, but you decide to let it go and move ahead. Let me be clear, this does not mean you should not protect yourself from people who try to take advantage of you or remove yourself from certain environments. It just means you chose not to hold onto the offense and therefore not be held captive by the offense yourself.

I believe this is your time to move forward and let go of the past, so let's start by breaking the stronghold of unforgiveness. Many authors have written great books about forgiveness and I don't want to rewrite what's already been written. Although I do want to share what I believe are some very powerful, yet practical, observations about forgiveness. If you haven't already read Matthew 18:21-35, take some time to read it now and let's identify some critical observations about the benefits of forgiveness, as well as some consequences of unforgiveness.

9 Observations about Forgiveness

1. <u>Forgiveness is not a one-time test, it's a life style:</u> Forgiveness is not situational or predicated on the offense; it's a God-like characteristic that all believers should consistently exhibit. We see in Matthew 18:21-22, when Peter asked the question, how many times shall I forgive my brother? Jesus didn't give a number that would be easy to remember. This is because He does not want us to have a number that when it's reached, frees us to hold a grudge forever. Seventy times seven means don't remember the number; remember the mandate to live the life of a forgiver.

2. <u>Your sin is not too big for God to forgive:</u> This is a very important concept to internalize, because without this understanding, many of us will feel like we have made such terrible mistakes that God will never take us back. We read in Chapter One that nothing could separate us from the love of God and that includes our sin. It does not matter how bad your mistake may be, just lay your burdens at the feet of your Savior, ask for forgiveness and He will forgive your sin.

3. God forgives those who ask, we must forgive whether it's asked for or not: God is always willing to forgive us of our sin. But He also teaches us to be more like Him by making sure we are aware of our behavior that is not like His. This is why God requires us to ask for forgiveness before He forgives us. 1John 1:9 tells us, *If we confess our sins, he is faithful and just to forgive us our sins, and to cleanse us from all unrighteousness.* God wants to make sure we know what we did wrong, admit what we did wrong and then make a decision not to continue doing wrong. By confessing our sin we make it clear to God that we agree, understand and openly acknowledge our error. God also understands the damage that unforgiveness can do in the life of the one holding on to an offense. This is why He requires us to forgive an offense committed against us even if the person that offended us never shows remorse, repents for their action or asks for our forgiveness.

4. God requires you to do for others what he has already done for you: Because Jesus is our example we must always emulate His ways above the worlds way of doing things. The worldly version of the golden rule is to do unto others as you would have them to do unto you. The Godly version says, do unto others as God has already done unto you, which means if God has forgiven us we must forgive others.

5. Your willingness to forgive others is a major component in God's requirements for Him to forgive you: is a major component in God's requirements for Him to forgive you. God is bound by His Word and if the Word says God can't forgive you unless you forgive others. He can't cut you a special deal based on what others have done to you. It won't work when you go to God and say; "They really hurt me so I should get a break on this forgiveness thing". God's Word is clear, we must forgive in order to be forgiven. I remember when I first really understood this. I felt it was so unfair of God to require me to forgive someone who didn't seem to be bothered at all about what they had done to me. My early application of this was not very spiritual but it was the best I could do at that time. I used to tell myself - they hurt me once by what they did and if I didn't forgive them I would assist them in continuing to hurt me by separating me from God. Especially since God is the source of my healing from the pain they originally caused. By not forgiving, I stay stuck to the place of pain and extend the healing process which ultimately produces more pain than the offense. If someone slapped you in the face, the pain from the slap could be gone in an hour. But if you refuse to forgive, that same slap could still be causing pain in your life five years later.

6. <u>Forgiveness helps to keep you in the right relationship with God and others:</u> Forgiveness is a critical key in maintaining healthy relationships because it allows us the opportunity to gracefully move past the offenses that will come. Forgiveness keeps us from staying stuck on the mistakes, missteps or mishaps that happen in all relationships. Forgiveness doesn't mean we are alright with what happened, it means we are alright to move forward in spite of what happened. It is because we understand that division destroys destiny.

7. <u>Forgiveness frees you from the place of pain:</u> The place of pain is the action, attack or offense that was the original source or cause of the pain. For example, if you were experiencing pain from having burned your foot three days earlier while walking on a hot surface with no shoes, the place of pain would be the original contact with the hot surface. Now, common sense would tell us, if we continue to walk over the hot surface without protecting ourselves we would most certainly re-aggravate the original wound and potentially cause new damage to our feet. Forgiveness in this case would be the equivalent of putting a protective covering over your feet. This would give you the ability to have exposure to the original source of pain while at the same time experiencing healing without running the risk of additional damage.

8. <u>Forgiveness breaks the hold the person that harmed you has</u>

over you: Believe it or not when you hold a grudge against someone you allow them to hold you in a suspended state of bondage. How many times have you tossed and turned at night because you were still angry about what someone did or said to you earlier that day. This is because your unwillingness to forgive enables that person to impact your feelings, focus and forward motion as it pertains to your ability to let go and move forward. And just for the record, that person, if the offense was intentional was probably sleeping like a baby. Other evidence of this is when exposure to people who you have not forgiven, adversely affects your mental, physical and spiritual well-being by changing your mood from glad and rejoicing, to mad and potentially responding in unhealthy ways.

9. Forgiveness helps to restore the person that harmed you: This is especially true when the offense was unintentional or when repentance has taken place. When someone you are in a relationship with unintentionally offends you, your response will determine his or her subsequent level of comfort as the relationship continues. If you say or show you have forgiven them and your actions correspond, they will feel that the relationship is back on track and able to freely move forward. On the contrary if you don't forgive, that relationship will be stuck at the point of pain, and the offender will most likely feel guilt and apprehension about the current and future state of the relationship.

Key observations about unforgiveness

To make sure you understand the benefits of forgiveness let's take a look at some consequences of unforgiveness.

Unforgiveness keeps you from being forgiven: It's worth taking the risk of sounding redundant to make sure this point is clear. God cannot and will not forgive you of your sins, committed against Him, if you are not willing to forgive others of offenses committed against you.

Unforgiveness hinders prayer, and limits God from freely moving on your behalf: Anytime we are disobedient toward the Word of God it is sin. So if God's Word tells us to forgive and we don't, we are in willful disobedience; and that is called sin. Psalms 66:18 says *"If I had ignored my sins, the Lord would not have listened to me"*. This tells us if we ignore or refuse to address our sin, God will refuse to listen to us, thereby rejecting our prayers. Mark 11:25 goes so far as to tell us, even before we start to pray we should first check our hearts to make sure we are not harboring unforgiveness or holding grudges against our brother. This means just what it says; if we start praying and are holding onto unforgiveness, God will not hear or respond to our prayers. This may be the very reason many prayers go unanswered and why many people actually feel as if their prayers never leave the room. Understand that unforgiveness is an act of disobedience that separates us from God.

Unforgiveness puts you outside the will and the protection of God: There is literally a gap or hole in your relationship with God when you are walking in unforgiveness. It leaves you uncovered and defenseless against the enemy's attacks: Romans 6:23 tells us that the wages of sin is death, which means the pay or the recompense we will receive for our sinful behavior is death. Death in the literal sense is when we die physically; death in the figurative sense is when we lose our ability to fulfill the purpose we were created to fulfill. Thus we render ourselves useless to God and forfeit the opportunity to live an abundant life. 1John 4:10 (CEV*)* says *"Real love isn't our love for God, but his love for us. God sent his Son to be the sacrifice by which our sins are forgiven."* This means we no longer have to pay the sin debt. Jesus paid for our sin with His own life, so we could live debt free. In Matthew 18:32-34 the servant who was unwilling to forgive was turned over to the torturers until he could pay his debt. This means when we refuse to forgive others we also refuse to receive our forgiveness and thus negate the price Jesus paid on the cross. We reassume the original debt for our own sin, which is death. By doing this we voluntarily disconnect ourselves from God and reconnect ourselves to the tormentor; Satan. We forfeit our authority over the devil and lose our ability to resist him, and we literally - not figuratively, become his prisoner. This is even more frightening when you consider God is the one who turns us over to the tormentor. The very same God who would normally rescue you is the same God who released you to the tormentor. Yes God still loves you, but he can't go against His Word and rescue you from the tormentor until the condition of your heart changes and you decide to forgive.

Unforgiveness will delay or even prevent healing sought through prayer: As we read earlier in Psalms 66 if we cry out to God for help, yet ignore and refuse to address the sin in our lives, God will not hear or respond to our prayers. What's the first thing we do when we get sick? We pray for healing. Well, if God doesn't hear or respond to our prayers for healing, and no natural method can be found, we just stay sick.

Unforgiveness is a cause of sickness and death: Most churches I have attended take communion numerous times throughout the year and most of them quote 1Corinthian11:27-32, which says *"Wherefore whosoever shall eat this bread, and drink this cup of the Lord, unworthily, shall be guilty of the body and blood of the Lord. ²⁸But let a man examine himself, and so let him eat of that bread, and drink of that cup. ²⁹For he that eateth and drinketh unworthily, eateth and drinketh damnation to himself, not discerning the Lord's body. ³⁰For this cause many are weak and sickly among you, and many sleep"*. Although it is not my intention to explain this fully it's important that you at least gain a basic understanding of these verses in context with this lesson.

Jesus' blood was shed and His body was broken as a sacrificial offering for our sin. Communion is our taking the time to remember and properly regard what Jesus did, why He did it and for whom He did it. To take communion or the Lord's Supper unworthily is to have an irreverent and careless attitude toward this sacred ordinance. Therefore, there is no room for callousness or division in the body of believers or carelessness in the mind of those partaking in communion that could in any way profane this sacred institution. Anyone who does not carefully examine themselves to make sure their heart is right toward Christ and the body of believers He gave His life for, runs the risk of being found unworthy and subject to judgment. Which, in this case, could bring sickness, weakness or death to the participant.

Unforgiveness causes isolation and division in the Body: Unforgiveness is one of the leading causes of division in the body of Christ and in personal relationships. It creates a division that weakens our ability to function as one voice, unified, serving one God. The devil has fooled many believers into actually thinking that they can be in right relationship with God and be walking in willful unforgiveness with each other. Romans 16:17 tells us that anyone who causes trouble and creates division in the body should be avoided. We are to protect ourselves from those who are walking in unforgiveness by not getting so close that we are drawn in and become participants of this self-defeating, body-dividing behavior.

Unforgiveness permanently ruins relationships: I personally have seen families, friendships, and marriages end under the pretense of being offended. The truth is many of those relationships were not ended because of the offense, but because of an unwillingness to forgive and move forward with the relationship.

Unforgiveness keeps you connected to the place of pain: Unforgiveness places you in a self-imposed prison, constantly reconnecting you to the original source of the pain. It creates a movie room in your mind that plays the same video clip over and over of something that happened to you in the past; sometimes many years ago. Because the clip is so clear and vivid, every time you replay it you relive the event, the physical pain and the emotional trauma by reconnecting yourself to it. Think of unforgiveness like a cut that won't heal because you keep pulling the scab off and picking at the wound, thus slowing down or completely stopping the healing process.

Unforgiveness causes you to live your present situations with a past-tense mentality: It takes all your old pains into every new opportunity. Luke 9:62 (AMP) *Jesus said to him, No one who puts his hand to the plow and looks back [to the things behind] is fit for the kingdom of God.* In other words, when you keep looking back, subconsciously what you're saying is, your past is more important than what God is trying to do now in your life. God wants to take us from glory to glory, so never make what you've been through more important than where God is currently taking you. When your past is allowed to become more important than your future, your past will most likely become your future.

Unforgiveness creates a stronghold: Unforgiveness is one of the biggest strongholds in the body of believers for two reasons. One, we all have been hurt, and two, most believers don't understand that unforgiveness closes the door on God while opening the door to satan. The result is the impartation of ungodly thoughts and the justification of ungodly actions and attitudes toward others. The word 'stronghold' comes from the Greek word – "ochuroma", which means "a castle, fortress, anything on which one relies or the arguments and reasonings by which a disputant endeavors to fortify his opinion and defend it against his opponent". So, in essence, a stronghold is something that holds you strongly to a place, position or a premise while resisting all outside input. This stronghold could be the result of any lie, false doctrine, or mindset that has created a fortified wall around your mind with the expressed intentions of keeping out truth, healing, restoration and deliverance. Simply put, a stronghold is something that keeps you locked in and keeps God locked out. Unforgiveness creates a fortified wall that holds you to the source of pain while holding out God; the source of deliverance and healing from that pain.

Proverbs 28:26 (AMP) tells us that "*He who leans on, trusts in, and is confident of his own mind and heart is a [self-confident] fool, but he who walks in skillful and godly Wisdom shall be delivered*".

If you believe your heart and mind when it tells you you've been hurt too bad to forgive; you are a self-confident fool. The truth is, you have been hurt too bad not to forgive and subsequently pull down that stronghold that keeps you locked in the place of pain. It keeps you separated from the deliverance you so desperately desire. The only way you can get deliverance from the source of pain and start the healing process, as simple as it may sound, is to forgive. Forgiveness does not mean you will instantly stop hurting, however, it is the place where the healing process begins.

Because unforgiveness is such a deceptive stronghold, it is not only important for us to understand it; we also need to be able to identify it in our lives and in the lives of other believers. Listed below are some common indicators or signs of a person walking in unforgiveness.

Prayers aren't being answered: If you feel you can't get a prayer through, when you start going through your checklist looking for possible hindrances, ask God to search your heart to see if there is any unforgiveness.

Peace is easily interrupted in certain situations or around certain people: When we find our peace is interrupted around certain people with whom we've had issues in the past that we have forgiven, this is often an indicator that forgiveness has taken place in our head but not in our hearts.

Prone to illness: Unforgiveness fractures your spiritual connection to God and godliness and breaks down your body's ability to properly handle stressful situations. The Bible says *"A merry heart doeth good like a medicine: but a broken spirit drieth the bones"* Proverbs 17:22. This means unforgiveness eats you up from the inside out and breaks down your body's natural ability to heal itself.

Unprovoked outbursts of anger or violence: If you find yourself angry and can't identify an external or current source for your anger there must be an internal source driving this emotion. If nothing has just happened, you must be responding to something that happened at another time in the past. Also if you find yourself regularly making mountains out of molehills, it's because you are not responding to molehills, you are responding to the mountain that your unforgiveness has built.

Often brings up past hurts or harms during unrelated conversations: Do you know anyone who, no matter what kind of new opportunities or blessings are currently impacting their lives, their focus always goes back to the past. Almost every conversation somehow turns into a "do you remember when somebody done me wrong?" song. Understand, it's not that this person wants to stay in the past; they just can't get out because they are still looking for some type of external resolution through an act of repentance from the perpetrator. And that, more than likely, is not going to happen.

Feels like you are stuck and you can't move or grow spiritually: Remember, unforgiveness puts you in the debtor's prison, which restricts your spiritual and emotional movement.

According to scripture, forgiveness in and of itself is not a process. It's a personal decision to respond in obedience to the Word of God. However, developing the mindset of a forgiver is a process that will make the act of obedience less of a struggle. I believe the inability of a believer to forgive is usually rooted in pride or a lack of faith in God. Pride tells you that you have a right to do what you feel and that you know what's best for you even when it goes against God's Word. Pride allows you to stare an absolute truth in the eye and then rationalize why it does not, or should not, apply to your situation. A lack of faith on the other hand will make you believe that the power of God has limitations when it comes to helping you overcome the pain the offense has caused. This is often someone who has yet to develop an intimate relationship with Christ outside of a church or group environment. This person really does not believe that God's grace is sufficient and that He loves them so much that their grieving grieves Him. They don't have a history of trusting God where a confidence in His faithfulness would have been developed.

As I stated earlier, forgiveness itself is not a process, but in many cases developing the mindset of a forgiver is. I want to close out this chapter by helping you develop the mindset of the forgiver. It's important that you establish some proper preparation thoughts, application thoughts and expectation thoughts for forgiveness. My prayer is that you will rehearse the following thoughts in your head until they drop down into your heart and govern your mind on forgiveness.

Preparation Thoughts, Before you Forgive:

- Do you understand that to willfully stay in unforgiveness is to willfully stay in sin and separation from God?
- Ask yourself, is this offense you're holding onto worth sacrificing your relationship with God?
- Do you fully understand that harboring unforgiveness toward others is an intentional decision to forfeit God's forgiveness toward you?
- Do you really believe God's grace is sufficient?
- If disobedience is the ultimate destiny destroyer, do you want to sacrifice your destiny?
- Remind yourself that forgiveness is God's way of protecting you from your carnal nature, and God's way of keeping the body of Christ from devouring itself from the inside out.

Application Thoughts: When I Forgive

- Take time to understand that your act of forgiving is one of the highest Christ like character traits a believer can display. *(Phi 2:2-5, Ep 4:17-32)*
- Forgiving means that you are ready to let go of the pain, get out of the prison and let God start the healing process.

Expectation Thoughts: After I Forgive

- Forgiveness doesn't mean you will immediately stop feeling the pain but it is the place where the healing process begins.
- Forgiveness won't change the facts or what happened to you, but it will change your focus, your fellowship with God, your feelings and your future.
- There is no hurt that God can't heal, therefore be confident God will get you through this because His grace is sufficient.

Always remember, your past may not let you go, but that doesn't mean you have to hold on to it. Break the stronghold, get out of that self-imposed prison and live your life believing that where God is taking you is worth letting go of the past.

Chapter 6:

Renewing the Mind

I beseech you therefore, brethren, by the mercies
of God, that ye present your bodies a living sacrifice,
holy, acceptable unto God, which is your reasonable
service. [2]And be not conformed to this world: but
be ye transformed by the renewing of your mind,
that ye may prove what is that good, and acceptable,
and perfect, will of God. Romans 12:1-2

In Chapter 5 we talked about forgiveness and the need to develop the mindset of the forgiver. In this chapter we expand the focus from a single aspect of our thinking to the actual transformation of our minds. Romans 12:1-2 are what I call progressive verses, because they explain the progression of getting from where you are, to where God desires you to be and they also explain the process that God has provided to get you there. If we look at the end of verse 2 it tells us God's desire is for us to prove His perfect will for our lives. But when you go back to verse one Paul tells us where the process starts and then lays out the progression to fulfillment. Paul tells us the first thing we need to do is present our bodies as a living sacrifice to God. Then he tells us not to be conformed to this world. The progression is finished by telling us to be transformed by the renewing of our mind. Before we take a closer look at the process let's look at three key words in the text and then establish some foundational thoughts around them.

The first key word is 'mind'. This is the Greek word "nous" which is "the intellectual faculty and the understanding". The contextual definition is "the place where our thoughts are received, and processed before corresponding actions are determined".

Simply put, the mind is the place where thoughts are formed, deliberated and decisions are made.

The second key word is 'renew'. This is the Greek word "anakainosis" which means "a renewal, renovation, or complete change for the better". The contextual definition is "to make new and better by way of fresh supply". When you renew something you pull out the old parts and practices and replace them with new ones that either allow it to work like new, better than new or do more than it was previously able to do.

The last key word is 'transform'. This is the Greek word "metamorphoo", it means "to change into another form, or transfigure". The contextual definition is "to keep the same basic foundation, but through the process of adding or removing certain components, you change appearance and/or function". In other words, your mind is still the place where thoughts are received and processed; but when you change how it processes by changing the filter that it uses, you change what it has the capability of producing.

Foundational Thoughts

Everyone has a preexisting criterion or mindset that currently determines how you process and respond to the thoughts that you think and receive in your mind. It is through this preexisting criterion or mindset that all incoming information is filtered, or processed through. In most cases this preexisting criterion has been formed by your environment, along with the influence others have had on your life, coupled with your personal life experiences. These factors are gleaned from the world and have become the foundations for the precepts, perspectives and principles that currently govern your life. Think about it; if your mind has a certain filter that it uses to process every thought and let's just say that filter is blue. Everything that gets poured into that filter will become blue. And it doesn't matter how clear, untainted or true it is at the beginning. Let's take this one step further this time; let's not use the color blue but the emotion blue. You hear a word that has the potential to give you hope in a seemingly hopeless situation, and that word is processed through that blue filter. You will not be able to respond to the word that went in the filter, only to the word that came out. It means you will still feel blue. This is not to say whether you are a good or bad person, it simply says we all start with a preexisting criterion based on a worldview and until that worldview has been transformed, we will never be able to prove God's vision, plan and purpose for our lives.

It is important to note here that even though we think and process information on different educational and experiential levels, no matter how elevated we are in our thinking, our minds must be purposely and biblically transformed. If not, the preexisting criteria that we have in place will still be adapted from the worlds system.

You will never be able to consistently change the way you act until you change the way you think, because your actions are your thoughts on display. So when we talk about renewing the mind, we're talking about the process of changing and transforming your way of thinking and processing information. We're talking about abandoning the preexisting criterion based on the world system and adopting new criteria based on biblical thinking or a Christ-like mindset. This happens when you systematically allow the spirit, word, and power of God to elevate, renovate, change, and grow your mind to the place where biblical truth overrides your past precepts, perspectives, principles and experiences.

Carnal Minded vs. Spiritual Minded

There are two basic mindsets believers operate from, carnal minded or spiritual minded. 'Carnal' comes from the Greek word "sarkikos" which means "having the nature of flesh, governed by mere human nature not by the Spirit of God and pertaining to the flesh". Simply put, a carnal minded believer is a person who has accepted Jesus as Lord, yet their thoughts, actions and attitudes are still influenced and governed by the world and their flesh. This carnal minded believer was precisely who Paul was talking to when he wrote *"And I, brethren, could not speak unto you as unto spiritual, but as unto carnal, even as unto babes in Christ. ²I have fed you with milk, and not with meat: for hitherto ye were not able to bear it, neither yet now are ye able. ³For ye are yet carnal: for whereas there is among you envying, and strife, and divisions, are ye not carnal, and walk as men?"* (1Corinthians 3:1-3) Paul is talking to believers who have experienced Christ and been taught the Word of God, yet are still operating under the influence of the flesh. This tells us that we can be in church sitting under good teaching and still be operating under the preexisting criterion gleaned from the world. This further illustrates that a transformed mind will not come by osmosis, proximity or seniority. So if you have been in church for the last twenty years but have not personally made the decision to renew your mind and transform your thinking, your mind has not been transformed. Sitting under the Word will definitely change you but only submitting to the Word will transform you.

Romans 8:5-8 gives us additional understanding of the difference of carnal minded vs. spiritual minded thinking when it says *"For they that are after the flesh do mind the things of the flesh; but they that are after the Spirit the things of the Spirit. ⁶For to be carnally minded is death; but to be spiritually minded is life and peace. ⁷Because the carnal mind is enmity against God: for it is not subject to the law of God, neither indeed can be. ⁸So then they that are in the flesh cannot please God"*. This reinforces the fact that an un-renewed or carnal mind still operating under the influence of the flesh, will be severely hampered in its ability to submit, serve and please God because of its inability to stop serving and pleasing itself. Although I believe we've already made this point clear it warrants repeating - if your mind has not been renewed it is still un-renewed. Let's take this a step further by identifying some of the more common characteristics of an un-renewed mind or carnal mindedness.

A carnal minded believer will receive, retain and focus on thoughts that are contrary to godliness when they are comforting to the flesh. Proverbs 23:7a says *"For as he thinketh in his heart, so is he"*. This tells us that the ungodly thoughts received in our heads, that we hold on to and focus on, will seat themselves in our heart and generate an action that is in line with the thought. This is why 2Corinthians 10:5 tells us that we should always be engaging in *"Casting down imaginations, and every high thing that exalteth itself against the knowledge of God, and bringing into captivity every thought to the obedience of Christ."* It's our job to cast down the ungodly thoughts before they take us down an ungodly path. Although we may not have control over the thoughts that pop into our heads for a visit we do have control over which thoughts we allow to reside.

A carnal minded believer will remain a slave to sin because they will yield to the flesh, rather than overcoming and taking control of the flesh. The Bible tells us that no good thing comes from the flesh. This means our flesh will never be a willing participant in our spiritual endeavors, so when we yield our thinking to the dictates of our flesh it will always lead us away from the directions of God. As long as you are yielding to your flesh you will never be able to maintain consistency in your spiritual walk.

A carnal minded believer will experience a dulling or reduced ability to sense the presence of God and comprehend the Word of God. When this condition exists you won't be able to hear from God with any kind of consistency. You will have trouble getting a personal revelation when the Word goes forth and normally you will not feel the presence and power of God at home or at church. Remember what Paul told the carnal minded Christians in 1 Corinthians 3:2 *"I have fed you with milk, and not with meat: for hitherto ye were not able to bear it, neither yet now are ye able"*. Paul is saying these believers can only receive baby revelation because their carnal mindedness or preexisting criterion is preventing them from becoming mature believers. The ability to perceive and achieve the will of God is contingent on the condition of your mind.

As we can see, Paul makes a distinction between carnal mindedness and spiritual mindedness. In Philippians 2:5 he makes this distinction even clearer when he tells us to *"Let this mind be in you, which was also in Christ Jesus"*. This is a very important scripture in context with this point because it gives us Christ Jesus as our working model for spiritual mindedness. Romans 8:6 says *"For to be carnally minded is death; but to be spiritually minded is life and peace."* The word 'spiritually' (minded) used here is Greek the word "pneuma" – which means "the third person of the triune God - the Holy Spirit". Spiritual mindedness is having your mind connected to, governed by and under the authority of the Spirit, Word and will of God. We see examples of this throughout scripture in the life of Jesus. In John 8:28 Jesus tells us that He does nothing on His own authority and speaks only what the Father has taught Him. In John 5:30 Jesus tells us again that He does nothing on His own but only the will of the Father which sent Him. We also see this at the Mount of Olives in Luke 22:42 where Jesus kneeled down and prayed *"Saying, Father, if thou be willing, remove this cup from me: nevertheless not my will, but thine, be done"*.

Again, when we are talking about transforming our minds using Jesus as our example, we're talking about systematically allowing the spirit, word, and power of God to elevate, renovate, change, and grow our minds. Our minds should grow to the place where the priorities, practices and predetermined patterns identified in the life of Christ become the new precepts, perspectives and principles that all incoming information received in the mind is filtered through. This is having your mind transformed by taking on the mind of Christ. In order to take on the mind of Christ you first need to have a basic understanding about the preexisting criterion or filter that governs the mind of Christ.

Our priorities determine the order of importance, what we put first or what we deem to be of the greatest value. Jesus' priorities were always clear in everything He did. His highest concern was the will of the Father coming to pass in every situation. In Matthew 6, Jesus instructs us to also make God's priorities our priorities by seeking the kingdom (rule and reign) of God first, (V.33) and to pray for God's will to be done in earth as it is in heaven (V.10). This makes it very clear that we are to always prayerfully seek God's plan and purpose in every situation we encounter. So by establishing the will of God as a priority in our thinking we will learn to hold on to thoughts that perpetuate God's kingdom in our lives and the lives of others.

The Bible also tells us that Jesus Christ is the same yesterday, today and forever which means; He does not vary but has a predetermined standard or pattern that He follows. 1Corinthians 14:40 tells us to *"Let all things be done decently and in order"*. Everything we do, including thinking, should have a predetermined pattern or order of succession that we follow. Once you have made a decision to make God's priorities yours, then every thought that enters your head should go through a predetermined set of checks and balances. This is how you will determine which thoughts line up with the Word and which thoughts don't.

When thoughts or ideas pop into your head that you are unsure about, quickly ask yourself - does that thought help you to seek and save the lost, destroy the works of the devil or help you or others to live the abundant life that Jesus made available? Do you see biblical principles? Does it line up with the plans and prophecies that God has revealed for your life? If the answer is yes; you act on the thoughts. If the answer is no; you cast them down. I guarantee, if you make God's priorities yours and follow this simple, yet powerful predetermined pattern, your life will be forever changed for the better. Let's return to our foundational scripture and take the first step in renewing your mind.

Step 1 - Presenting your bodies as a living sacrifice

Paul writes in Romans 12:1 "*I beseech you therefore, brethren, by the mercies of God, that ye present your bodies a living sacrifice, holy, acceptable unto God, which is your reasonable service*". This means we are to offer the way we live as a sacrifice to God, giving up the right to choose for ourselves. I believe this first step is the most important of the three-step process of transforming your mind and thought patterns for three significant reasons. First, it places God on the throne of your life by making Him Lord. Second, it solidifies your willingness to live for Him and not yourself. Third, it eliminates self and world sufficiency.

One of the key reasons many believers have not had their minds transformed is because it's not something initiated or forced by God. This is something that you must see in scripture, then decide on your own to do. Paul says we are to present our bodies which means this is voluntary or of our own volition. God will not force you to do this. You can't wait for God to make this happen. Isaiah 55:6 tells us to "*Seek ye the LORD while he may be found, call ye upon him while he is near*". Jeremiah 29:13 says "*And ye shall seek me, and find me, when ye shall search for me with all your heart*". This assures us that God is available to be found but we must be looking for Him and not just waiting. This has to be a decision that's rooted in an overwhelming love and desire to serve God, please God and be all He desires for you to be. This is not a decision that God or anybody else can make for you. This decision is totally up to you.

The word 'sacrifice' used in Romans 12:1 is "thuo", which means "to kill, or to make sacrificial offerings by killing". So you kill or sacrifice the things that you feel are important to you, and become willing to die to your dreams, your plans, and your desires for yourself in order to receive and fulfill God's plan for your life. This willing sacrifice validates God as a priority and gives you the ability to live for Him. There are three key elements in this sacrifice that warrant explanation:

In order for a sacrifice to be valid it must meet the preexisting requirements: We don't get to give God whatever we want and expect Him to accept it. That's not the way it works as we can see in the story of the rich young ruler found in Luke 18:18-25. I chose this story to illustrate the first point because the ruler was doing everything he thought was right based on his preexisting criterion. He was keeping the commandments; not committing adultery, not stealing, lying or dishonoring his father or mother. I don't want to minimize this because it is how we all should live. But, I do want to emphasize that this was not a sacrifice to the ruler because it did not cost him anything he felt he had a right or entitlement to have. The ruler had been raised to be honest, respectful and obedient so it was not considered a sacrifice to him. On the contrary, he had also been raised in a wealthy environment which I believe he felt was an entitlement that gave him power and position in society. His wealth was where he got his security, personal value and means to fulfill the dreams and desires he held close. Jesus knew the only real sacrifice for the ruler was to give up the security of his riches and become a servant to the Savior. We see that this was a sacrifice the ruler was not willing to make, and we also see that Jesus would not accept anything less. This clarifies the fact that we don't get to decide what sacrifice to make, we only get to decide if we are willing to make the sacrifice that Jesus requires.

A living sacrifice has to be alive at the point of sacrifice and continue to live during the sacrifice: In contrast to a standard Levitical offering, where an animal was selected, slain and submitted as the sacrifice, in a living sacrifice man selects himself as the sacrifice. He slays his personal desires and submits the works of his body to an ongoing standard of holiness established by God. I believe the simplest and most practical way to understand this is to look at the five senses of the body and sacrifice each of them for Godly use. Your touch, taste, smell, sight and hearing should all be used as a sacrifice to God. For example, to touch is to make contact, handle or impact. Therefore, everything we touch should be touched with the intent to produce God's desired outcome. To taste is to perceive or distinguish flavor and or contents. Anything we are not sure about we should taste or test it first to make sure it lines up with the Word and will of God before we indulge ourselves in it. When we offer our body as a living sacrifice to God, our senses should be working in harmony to protect us from falling into the trappings of the world while perceiving, promoting and producing God's will for our lives.

Offering your bodies as a living sacrifice is also different from the Levitical offering in the sense that once a sacrifice was made, it could not be reversed. A living sacrifice is not a one-time deal; it's an ongoing lifestyle that is consistently committed to Godliness. This means at the point that your commitment to God drops off, so does your status as a living sacrifice. Remember in 1 Corinthians 9:27 Paul said he had to keep his body under and bring it into subjection. This means it takes constant effort and extreme discipline to maintain the level of self-denial a living sacrifice requires. A living sacrifice only continues living or producing when it continues dying and denying itself. A living sacrifice starts with willingness and is maintained through obedience thus becoming a tool for the use of the master builder.

Step 2 – And be not conformed to this world

Not only is the presentation of our bodies the subject of Paul's request, it is the pattern of our behavior as noted in the statement *"be not conformed to this world"*. Paul cautions the believer not to be fashioned after this world or age. The world system of this age is an evil one (Gal 1:4), and is dominated by "the god of this world" (2 Corinthians 4:4). The new creation in Christ is to live with the understanding that *"old things are passed away; behold, all things are become new"* (2 Corinthians 5:17). We are therefore not to continue to have our lives governed by the thought patterns and dictates of this evil world system. This means after you make the decision to live for God you punctuate that decision by disconnecting yourself from the world's way of thinking and acting. You decide to be different from the world system by developing and implementing a lifestyle that strengthens you in the ways of God, while empowering you to resist the ways of the world which is governed by the god of this world; satan.

In essence, you change your current standards of living that are conformed to or based on the world's way of thinking and acting. The Bible tells us to be in the world but not of the world which means we are to function in the world by using a different set of standards. We are to act differently or be peculiar. We've already learned that if we are to act differently, we will need to change the way we think. And to change the way we think is to change the preexisting criterion that governs our thinking. We will need to change our priorities, preexisting notions, passed down patterns and personal proclivities. It won't be easy to go against the standards and practices that you, and those around you, have always viewed as acceptable. It won't be easy to stop doing things the way you have always done them or to break family and work place traditions that have brought you comfort and varying levels of success in the past.

For most believers, this will create what seems to be a void in your life. You may wonder, if I don't do what I have always done, then what will I do? You may even ask the question, does God really expect me to change right away? No, God does not expect you to change everything right away, He knows this is a process. The renewing of the mind takes place gradually and systematically over time. But this renewing process won't start until you decide to live for God and cease to conform to the world. Real change that transforms your actions is the external display of the transformation that has taken place first in your mind through your thinking. As we have already learned our actions are our internal thoughts on display. You will never be able to consistently change the way you act until you change the way you think.

The first critical key in not conforming to this world is to cultivate and implement a new value system based on what is pleasing and important to God. This means the Word of God must be your only barometer for measuring moral conduct and all information that enters your mind must be processed according to the Word and will of God. You must decide in your mind before you take action with your body what is Godly and what is not. Notice I didn't say what's good and what's not, I said what is Godly and what is not. You should understand that everything the devil and the world throws at you will not be sin. Some things will come at you to get you to lower your guard and your standards, so that sin can creep in at a later time.

I remember some years back, I was at work and there was an emergency that called for overtime. When I called my boss, who had no prior knowledge of the situation, I was told to take my time completing the job so it would last at least four hours. Once I had a crew on site I realized the job would only take about two hours or less. When I called my boss back, he still said make it last four hours or more. My dilemma was - should I make a two-hour job last four hours? Technically, this was not sin on my part because I was given a directive from my superior. The world system, per my boss - who by the way was also being paid time and-a-half, told me it was okay to milk taxpayer dollars. Now, I had long ago made the decision to live for God and everybody I worked with knew this, including my boss. For me there was actually no new decision to make in this case, I just had to enforce my existing decision to abide by God's standards and not conform to the world's standards.

Consequently we left when the job was done, which actually took less than two hours. It seemed no sooner than I had left the job, the Holy Spirit told me my boss was testing me to see if I would lower my standards this time. That way, the next time he asked me to lie or steal, if I said no, he could remind me there was no need to act holy because my integrity had already been compromised. On a side note, my boss was really upset with me, and though he could not write me up for insubordination, he mistreated me every chance he could. But God protected me and I later retired with full benefits, my boss eventually got fired.

When you decide not to conform to the world, you don't get removed from the world, you just respond to it differently. There are things in life you will always have to deal with. That means you must learn and implement new ways to handle those situations. Decisions produce results or consequences, so if I decide to change the way I respond to a situation, I change the outcome of that situation. The Lord God Himself spoke to Joshua saying *"This book of the law shall not depart out of thy mouth; but thou shalt meditate therein day and night, that thou mayest observe to do according to all that is written therein: for then thou shalt make thy way prosperous, and then thou shalt have good success"* (Joshua 1:8). Your success is not based on external circumstances; it's based on an internal decision to follow Word based principles in world-based situations. Think about it, Joshua was instructed to meditate or focus on the Word of God so strongly that he could not see himself doing anything contrary to it. In essence God was instructing Joshua how to function in the world while not being conformed to it by implementing a new value system. By using God's value system, "His Word" Joshua would please God, invoke the power of God and produce the purposes of God; thereby insuring Godly success in worldly environments. Remember, Godly actions in ungodly environments will produce Godly results in the life of the believer. This means when you stop conforming to the world you will stop the influence the world has on you and you begin to exercise the influence you, as a believer, are supposed to have on the world.

Step 3 - Be ye transformed by the renewing of your mind.

In this section we will focus on the renewing of your mind, which is what ultimately produces the transformed mind. Renewing is the process, and transformation is what the process is designed to produce. As noted in the definition, the word transform implies a foundational change in the believer's inward nature, which is followed by a pattern of character, and behavior that corresponds with that new nature. So, the center of logical reasoning, ethical judgment and moral awareness is completely changed. Also it should be noted that the transforming of your mind through the process of renewal is not a one-time event. It is an ongoing adventure that happens as new revelations are synthesized into your decision making process.

For example, you make a decision that you want to change how you treat your wife. In essence you have identified an external behavior that you want to transform. Because you know your actions are the reflections of your thinking and your thinking is driving your behavior, the only permanent solution is to change your thinking. This is where many counselors miss the mark. They focus all the attention on controlling the behavior or the symptoms, without focusing on the root cause. It is the preexisting criterion we have in our minds that has allowed us to believe the errant behavior was acceptable in the first place. Without the renewal of your mind on this matter you will only have will power, and will power is only as strong as the person willing the power. In other words, you will try to change your external actions without sufficient internal support which, usually, will not work for extended periods of time. In order to change or transform how you treat your wife you, should first change or transform how and what you think about your wife.

When Loretta and I first got married I was teaching an adult Sunday class and leading a men's ministry at our church. I had made a decision to live for God and not conform to the world's way of thinking and acting, and in many areas my mind had been transformed. I soon discovered that, although my mind had been transformed in other areas as it pertained to marriage, I still held on to a world view based on the environment in which I was raised.

I used to tell my wife that because I went to work and brought my money home, didn't drink, smoke or hang out, she should be happy. Even though I didn't show much affection or share my feelings or try to understand her emotional needs, I felt as long as I didn't lie or cheat, she had no reason to voice any displeasure in our relationship. It wasn't until we started attending Detroit World Outreach, pastored by the late Bishop Jack Wallace, and going to their men's ministry, MOV (Men of Valor), taught by Elder Ben Gibert that I started to understand God's perspectives on marriage. I remember the first time I went to MOV and Elder Ben asked the question "Who considers themselves to be the strong silent type in your marriage?" I boldly raised my hand expecting to be saluted. Then Elder Ben passionately declared there is no such thing as the strong silent type, only the strong stupid type.

He explained that a man who did not share his feelings with his wife ran the risk of letting her feel devalued, unsure about the relationship, emotionally unfulfilled and unappreciated as a help meet. I went home and told Loretta I was never going back to that place. When she asked me why and I told her what he called me and what he said about my actions, Loretta told me he was right about what he called me, how she felt and that I was wrong about not going back. Because Elder Ben gave scripture to back up what he said, I was forced to look at my behavior based on what was acceptable to God and not what was comfortable and acceptable to me. I began to search the scriptures for every verse that contained the words husband, wife and marriage. After meditating these scriptures I asked God to give me personal revelation on them, regarding my marriage. My perspectives on my role as a husband, and how God wanted me to treat my wife, changed. Although it took some time, once this new revelation became a part of my decision making process, my mind had been transformed and my actions followed my new perspectives.

As mentioned earlier in the chapter, transformation is to keep the same basic foundation, but through the process of adding or removing certain components, the appearance and the function changes. You keep the mind that you have, but because you strip out the worlds influence and renew it with the Words influence, it starts to function in line with God's will for you. Transforming your mind allows you to become a purpose-producing tool that God can use. With that thought fresh in your mind let's look at seven practical keys to a renewed way of thinking that will ultimately transform your mind.

1. Understand, God's desire is that we change because of revelation not fear:

Many believers are motivated by loss and not by love; or by pain and not by a personal commitment for better. This attitude or mindset plays right into the world's way of thinking, which says it's okay as long as you don't get caught or feel bad about what you are doing. You must make a decision that you want your life to be a valid reflection of Christ in the earth realm. This means as you get revelation of better, in any area of your life, you will automatically want to change because your first desire is to be pleasing to God.

2. Learn to guard and protect your mind:

Because our actions are reflective of our thinking, if we change the things we think about, we change the things we do. Philippians

4:8 tell us to think about things that are true, honest, just, pure, lovely, of good report, virtuous and praiseworthy. It will be a good project for you to study each one of these words and build an action plan around them. For example, let's look at the first word – 'true'. Things that are true are reliable, unfailing, sure, unconcealed and actual. This means we are to speak, walk in, declare, worship, believe, know, accurately handle, obey and be established by what we know to be true. Think of how focusing on just this one word could change your life. You would start focusing on the solutions, not the problems. You would establish yourself as the victor that the Bible says you are and not the role of victim you have erroneously accepted. You would stop focusing on the past and focus on the promises of God for your life. That means you could eventually become the problem solving, promise producing person that God created you to be.

My intention here is not to get you excited (although you should be), but to make sure you understand that transforming your mind or the way you think, will change your life. Ask yourself why God wants you to consistently think about specific things. It's so you can consistently produce specific responses that will produce the specific results God wants manifested in your life. Paul ends V. 8 with these words "think on these things" – let them become the object of your attention, and the meditation of your heart; the barometer of what is to come and the new standard for all thought.

3. Identify and eliminate sin in your life:

The simplest way to do this is to deal with the known sin in your life first. In other words, you should deal with what you already know is wrong. If it's something you feel you need to hide, it's probably wrong. Or if it's something you may not feel is wrong but you have received conviction from the Holy Spirit about, it's wrong. When I rededicated my life to Christ I knew smoking, drinking, getting drunk, drugging, lying and fornicating were wrong. I didn't need the Holy Spirit or the preacher to tell me that. Other things I learned later; some from reading the Word, hearing the Word or through conviction from the Holy Spirit. The point is this, some things will change over time, but some things just need to stop right now.

4. Always seek God's desired outcome in every situation (internal and external):

The Bible tells us that God is omniscient or that he knows everything that has happened, is happening or ever will happen to everybody and everything. Jeremiah 29:11 tells us that God has a plan and an expected end for each of our lives. This means God has a desired outcome for every situation that we face and when we seek his desired outcome in our current situations it keeps us following the plan that leads to God's expected end. Don't go into situations believing "whatever happens". Always set yourselves to expect and respond in a way that promotes God's desired outcome for your life and anyone else involved.

5. Get a clear picture in your mind of your desired pattern of thinking:

There needs to be certain thoughts or thought patterns that you train yourself to think. In solving a math problem there is a chronological order that you follow to solve the problem. You should adapt this same logic or formula as you are renewing your mind. This will keep you from reverting back to your old ways of thinking and responding. A simple formula that I use is the acronym R.A.S.E. which stands for Remind, Ask, Submit, and Expect.

- I **R**emind myself it's not about me it's about God's will being done.
- I **A**sk God to reveal His desired outcome for personal instruction.
- I **S**ubmit myself wholly to God's revealed will, and
- I **E**xpect God's purpose to come to pass.

This is based on Matthew 6:33 and serves as a self-check mechanism to keep my thinking decent, in order and in sync with the mindset of Christ.

6. Develop the habit of dropping all thoughts that are not conducive to transforming your mind:

Remember, Proverbs 23:7 tells us that as a man thinketh in his heart so is he, meaning any ungodly thought you allow to linger will eventually cause you to respond in line with the thought. This is why 2Corinthians 10:5 emphasizes the *"Casting down imaginations, and every high thing that exalteth itself against the knowledge of God, and bringing into captivity every thought to the obedience of Christ"*. If you don't cast down ungodly thoughts they will lead you to ungodly actions. Part of the process of renewing and transforming your mind is training yourself to identify ungodly thoughts instantly so as to minimize the potential of relapse into old behaviors.

7. Surround yourself with light and separate yourself from darkness:

It is very important that you monitor who and what is around you at all times. The company you keep will have a positive or negative impact on your life. Proverbs 13:20 says *" He that walketh with wise men shall be wise: but a companion of fools shall be destroyed."* This tells us that when we pattern our internal and external behavior after a wise man (one who understands and lives by Godly principles) we will become wise. This means you still learn by trial and error, it's just not your trial and error. As Godly men and women we don't have to guess what works and what doesn't, we can identify Godly men and women who are inheriting the promises of God and follow them to the same outcome. 1Corinthians 15:33 (MKJV) adds this to our point *"Do not be deceived; evil companionships corrupt good habits"*. Choose carefully who you fellowship with because you will be positively affected or negatively infected.

The other part of this is the importance of what you expose yourself to. Luke 11:34 says, *The lamp of the body is your eye. When your eye is sound, then your whole body is filled with light, but when it is bad, then your body is in darkness.* The things you take in through the eye will determine what's on the inside of you. If you fill yourself with light, or what is morally acceptable, you will become as the light. On the contrary, if you fill yourself with darkness you will become as one not able to reflect the light of God. That thing you have filled yourself with to this point in life determines the person you are now. The things you fill yourself with from this point forward will determine the person you will become. It's your right to choose. 3 John 2 says *"Beloved, I wish above all things that thou mayest prosper and be in health, even as thy soul prospereth"*.

This means the mind is the governor of the soul and the key to a prosperous life. Contrary to what some might think and even teach, God wants us to live a prosperous life, but as we can see in the verse above, God also wants this prosperity to be in balance with our ability to manage it properly. The key to external prosperity that is allowed and established by God is internal prosperity. Yes, John is telling His friend Gaius that his greatest wish is for him is to prosper. He goes on to tell Gaius that this prosperity or good external success is the by-product or the outward manifestation of the prosperity that must first take place in his soul.

We learned in Chapter 3 that the soul of man is made up of the mind, will, emotions, intellect and the imagination. In order for your soul to prosper and become the catalyst for overall prosperity, all of its elements, individually and collectively, must prosper. This means if your emotions are out of order, they will keep your soul from prospering and this works the same way with the other four elements of your soul. Each must prosper and continue to prosper in order for your soul to prosper.

The words 'prosper and prospereth' are the same word – "euodoō" which comes from compound words "Yoo" which means "good, well done and acting well"; and the word "Hod-os" which means "way side, journey, highway, traveled way, and road". Metaphorically, it means a course of conduct or manner of thinking, feeling and deciding. Our contextual definition for the phrase "as thy soul prospereth" is "the increasing alignment of the soul of man with the will of God". The increasing ability to enforce God's will into man's manner of thinking, feeling, deciding and conduct – thus allowing God's word to determine man's attitude, actions, expectations and outcomes in his journey through life. John understood that ongoing prosperity is not predicated on circumstances but on our ongoing ability to manage ourselves properly in the precepts and principles of God.

It is also important that you notice, this prosperity that John is talking about is not about money. It's actually much bigger than money because the implications are that we will have good success in the business of life. To really get this picture in your mind, a good project would be to go through the Bible and identify the things that God has deemed valuable. Things like wisdom, relationships, health, marriage, wealth, every good and perfect gift, God's promises and the list goes on. In case you're wondering what this has to do with the renewing of the mind – everything! The mind is the governor of the soul.

Years ago when I started driving trucks, one of the first things I noticed was the size, sound and power of the diesel engine. Once I got comfortable with the size of the trucks and started driving on the freeways I realized I couldn't get the truck to go over 55 miles per hour. No matter how hard I tried, it seemed that the power from the engine was not getting where it needed to go to make the truck run faster. I found out that the trucks had a device called a governor. The job of the governor is to determine how much power is allowed to go through. Let me be clear, the governor does not determine how much power is available, only how much of the available power is allowed to go through. Philippians 2:5 tells us to *"Let this mind be in you, which was also in Christ Jesus:"* Or we could say, "let us have the same mindset or pattern of thinking as Jesus", the emphasis being on the mind. And again, in our foundational verse for this lesson we learn that our ability to validate God's will for our lives is contingent on the condition of our mind.

I want you to see that your mind is the governor of your soul, and your soul's ability to prosper is contingent on the amount of God's perspective or power your mind allows to come through.

Let's walk through a real life situation, first in an un-renewed mind, then in a transformed mind so you can have a picture of how this works. So, you get a report from the doctor that says that you have cancer. You receive this information in your mind, which then involves the other elements of your soul to process the information and determine a course of action.

I believe this exchange goes as follows. After the mind receives the report it hands the information to the intellect. The intellect will present the facts back to the mind based on the relevant data it has. The intellect starts to remember everyone who died from that form of cancer, what treatment options are available and then relays it's concerns back to the mind. The mind evaluates these facts, then hands off to the emotions. The emotions look at the information and allows fear to start creeping in, bringing with it a feeling of helplessness that could lead to hopelessness. The mind takes what it has received from the intellect and the emotions and sends it to the imagination which begins forming a picture of what you will look like as this disease progresses through your body. Your mind now takes what it has learned from the intellect, what it feels from the emotions, what it sees through the imagination and gives its decision to the will (the minds enforcer).

Now let's look at this same scenario from a transformed mind. After receiving the information in your mind, you give it to your intellect. The intellect will only look at the facts to properly understand the situation, but then it knows to lean not to its own understanding because it knows that facts are not always the truth. So the intellect doesn't try to remember everyone that died from cancer; it remembers everyone that got delivered and healed from cancer. It searches itself for healing scriptures and faith confessions to give to the mind. The mind takes this information and hands it to the emotions, which sets and settles itself based on scriptural truth, not worldly data. It realizes that *"A sound mind makes for a robust body, but runaway emotions corrode the bones."* Proverbs 14:30 (MSG). After receiving the report back from the emotions, the mind turns to the imagination.

The imagination begins to cast down all thoughts and facts that don't line up with truth from God's word and begins to form a picture of health and prosperity based on the Word of God and faith in that Word. This is given back to the mind, which now tells the will to walk in victory through faith. Remember, all battles are spiritual and all spiritual battles are won in the soulish realm which is governed by the mind. Therefore I beseech you this day to be transformed by the renewing of your mind that you would be able to prove what is the good, acceptable and perfect will of God for your life.

Chapter 7:

Commitment

Trust in the LORD, and do good; so shalt thou
dwell in the land, and verily thou shalt be fed.
[4]Delight thyself also in the LORD; and he shall
give thee the desires of thine heart .[5] Commit thy
way unto the LORD; trust also in him; and he shall
bring it to pass. Psalms 37:3-5

Our focus in the last chapter was on the renewing of the mind. In this chapter we will focus on a key component in the renewal process; commitment. When your mind is renewed you have a new normal or new base line for your thinking patterns. This is brought about by your decision to see things differently, along with a commitment to continue the process of change until that new normal is established. Research shows that it takes about twenty-one days to develop a new habit. With this in mind, we can see why real change may start with a decision, but it can only be established by a commitment to follow through on that decision. This explains why many of us may have decided to change or be different on numerous occasions but, without a commitment to the process that produces change, it just didn't happen. Psalms 37:3-5 is what I call the path to commitment in that it introduces us to a biblical way in which true commitment can be established. It starts with trust, moves to delight and ultimately commitment. Commitment is a word that most adults know but very few really understand its power. As we go over the scriptures, the goal is to help you see and understand the path to commitment, principles of commitment and the biblical promises related to commitment.

The Path to Commitment

Trust in the LORD, and do good; so shalt thou dwell in the land, and verily thou shalt be fed. Psalms 37:3

Trust is the entry level or first step on the path to developing commitment. The word 'trust' used in this verse is the Hebrew word "baw-takh" which means "to be confident, bold or sure". Our contextual definition is "a confident reliance that produces a resting of the mind because of the integrity, veracity, justice, ability, relationship or other sound principles of another person". In essence, your trust in God is based on your confident awareness of His ability and faithfulness. In turn, it allows you to step out with some level of confidence, believing that God can and will do (for you) what His Word promises. Real trust should be the by-product of observed faithfulness, not something that should exist without a history of demonstrated consistency.

This verse also teaches us that when we trust God and that trust is validated by a corresponding action, God will move on our behalf. When our trust in God is followed by a Godly lifestyle which validates that trust, God will lead us to, or establish us in a place or state of being that He has prepared for us. The verse goes on to tell us that God will provide natural and spiritual provision in that land. God responds to your trust in Him by providing for your basic physical, mental and spiritual needs. It is this moving or responding to your trust in God that builds your hope, raises your expectation, confirms His love, and solidifies His power to keep His promises. Your ability to trust God continues to grow as a result of God's response to your current level of trust. Remember, this path to commitment was developed by God with the intent to lead us through trust, to delight and ultimately to commitment. Think about that for a moment. If God is the one who wants to build a level of commitment from us to Him, He has to respond to our trust in a way that shows His commitment to us. Thusly, making it safe for us to delight in Him and eventually able to commit. God understands that He has to meet you where you are, in order to lead you where He wants you to go. His faithful response to your trust and reliance on Him causes Him to become the center of your joy, the object of your affection and the source of unmatched fulfillment; your delight.

The second step on the path to commitment is delight. This means to be happy about, to make merry over or make sport of. Our contextual definition is "the source of great joy, pleasure, comfort and satisfaction". At this point we have progressed from merely trusting God to delighting in Him as well. We can also see a progression in how God responds to this new level of relationship we are developing with Him. Remember, in Psalms 37:3 God said if we trust in Him and do good we will dwell in the land and surely be fed. Again, this lets us know that God wants to supply for our basic needs. But as we grow from merely trusting God to delighting in Him, God moves from meeting our basic needs to granting our innermost desires. Psalms 37:4 tells us to *"Delight thyself also in the LORD; and he shall give thee the desires of thine heart"*. As you move from trusting in God to delighting in God, God moves from meeting your basic needs to granting the desires of your heart.

God can now trust you at a higher level of revelation and manifestation because He has become the center of your joy. True delight in God is not predicated on reliance for some particular thing, but purely on a reverential relationship that is formed after being exposed to the heart, love and provision of God that brings you to a place where you can find no real joy outside of His presence. This means when we consume ourselves with the desire to please God (when what pleases God becomes what pleases us), pleasing us becomes what pleases God. When we learn to be excited about the things of God and become devoted to the purposes of God, pleasing us and destiny fulfillment are one and the same. It means we have come to the point of wanting what God wants for us.

V.5 takes it to another level for you and for God. *"Commit thy way unto the LORD; trust also in him; and he shall bring it to pass*. This brings us to the last step on the path to commitment; commitment itself. The word 'commitment' used here is the Hebrew word "gâlal" which means "to roll oneself or wallow". Our contextual definitions are: "to roll to, hold firm, to make the last place or the willingness to do whatever is necessary to obtain something that is esteemed to have higher value". True commitment to God is rooted in the decision not to turn back, regardless of the situation or the consequences. This is when your desire to serve God outweighs all the physical, spiritual and soulish opposition you face. This is the place where God wants believers to be, at the point of no return. This means we have totally committed ourselves to accomplishing God's will for our lives.

As we saw in the first two verses, every time we step into a higher level of reliance and relationship with God, God responds by releasing a higher level of grace or empowerment into our lives. He went from meeting our basic needs to granting the desires of our heart to actually bringing it to pass Himself. The question at this point is, what is "it"? What is God actually bringing to pass in your life. Ephesians 2:10 (AMP) tells us *"For we are God's [own] handiwork (His workmanship), recreated in Christ Jesus, [born anew] that we may do those good works which God predestined (planned beforehand) for us [taking paths which He prepared ahead of time], that we should walk in them [living the good life which He prearranged and made ready for us to live]"*. This makes it clear that God has a preplanned purpose for our lives and also a prearranged good life, which is part of our reward for fulfilling that purpose.

Personally, I have known for years that God has a plan and purpose for my life, but what I didn't know was how it would come to pass. Again, Psalms 37:5 tells us when we commit to God and trust God, He brings it to pass. 'It' is God's preplanned, good works (purpose) and His prearranged good life (the fulfillment that comes from accomplishing what you were created to do). Let me be clear, when you commit to God, you commit to His purpose for your life, His plan for you and the path that is already prepared to get you to the place where God wants you to be. This is not magic, it is pliability in that you give God complete control to shape and steer your life. In other words any believer who commits their life to God has a guarantee from God Himself that the purpose for their life will be brought to pass. I know this is a powerful statement, but it is God's response to your powerful act of commitment. To help you see this even clearer, let's look at two principles related to commitment. First: when you commit your actions and the course of your life over to God He moves on His behalf - by moving on yours.

It was God's plan all the time. So, when you commit yourself to God's plan for your life and He moves on your behalf, He is also moving on His own behalf by helping you do what He created you to do. You see, when you commit to God, His plan and your plan become the same plan. Secondly; a life committed to God is not responsible for its destiny fulfillment. Once you commit to God, the end result of your life is no longer your responsibility because God said, "He will bring it to pass". This does not mean you get to take a seat and watch; this means your job is to stay pliable so God can continue to shape and steer you.

Ponder Point: When you commit your "what's" (the things you do) and your "why's" (the reason you do them) to God your blessings will run on automatic.

Let's examine some other examples of commitment in scripture.

Commitment in Action: 3 Case Studies

Daniel is a good example of one who started with God and stayed with God in the midst of an ungodly nation ruled by an ungodly king. Yet in the midst of it all, Daniel was committed. Our first case study will look at the life of Daniel.

And the king spake unto Ashpenaz the master of his eunuchs, that he should bring certain of the children of Israel, and of the king's seed, and of the princes; [4]Children in whom was no blemish, but well favoured, and skilful in all wisdom, and cunning in knowledge, and understanding science, and such as had ability in them to stand in the king's palace, and whom they might teach the learning and the tongue of the Chaldeans. Daniel 1:3-4

Although Daniel's whole life was one of consistency in his commitment to God, we're only going to focus on two accounts of commitment in this study. The verse above tells us that the king was looking for young men between fifteen and twenty years of age, with no physical, mental or moral defects. These young men needed to be skillful in Jewish laws, customs, religion, liberal arts and sciences with the potential to study, learn and retain the Babylonian culture. Scripture also indicates that Daniel had already committed to live his life according to the laws of God prior to being taken into captivity. We see evidence of this in Daniel 1:8 (CEV) when we read, *"Daniel made up his mind to eat and drink only what God had approved for his people to eat. And he asked the king's chief official for permission not to eat the food and wine served in the royal palace"*.

The king's plan for Daniel and the other young men was to eat and drink his chosen delicacies, learn from his best teachers and be evaluated after a period of three years. This seemingly kind gesture from the king challenged Daniel's commitment to God right from the beginning regarding what was acceptable for him to eat and drink. Daniel responded by convincing the guard to allow him to have only vegetables and water instead of the rich food and wine of the king for a period of ten days. Then they would compare his physical condition to the young men who had partaken of the king's regimen. This also shows us that commitment is constant and does not vacillate, even when it seems that compromise will produce a greater reward. It would have been simple for Daniel to eat the king's food not knowing how the guards would respond to his request. When we compromise, we cave into the pressure of the world but when we commit, we tap into the prevailing power of God. As we read in Daniel 1:15-16 (CEV) *"Ten days later, Daniel and his friends looked healthier and better than the young men who had been served food from the royal palace [16]After this, the guard let them eat vegetables instead of the rich food and wine"*

Next we turn our attention to Daniel 6. By this time Daniel was under his third king, Darius. King Darius set Daniel over the whole realm of his kingdom because an excellent spirit (the spirit of God) was in him. The governors and officials that Daniel had been appointed over sought to find fault with Daniel; but could not. He was faithful in all that he did so all that was left to attack was Daniel's faithfulness to his God. Knowing of Daniel's daily pattern of praying three times in front of the window that faced Jerusalem, they sought to use this against Daniel. The governors and officials convinced the king to establish a decree forbidding anyone to pray to or petition any God or human except King Darius himself for a period of thirty days. Anyone who would disobey this decree would be thrown into the lion's den.

After hearing of this decree Daniel returned home and prayed as he had always done. Once those looking to find fault in Daniel saw this, the king was notified immediately. Even though the king had great regard for Daniel he was bound by his written decree to throw Daniel into the lion's den. Yet, before throwing Daniel into the lion's den the king noted Daniel's faithfulness to his God and prayed his God would rescue him. The next day the king found that Daniel's God had honored his innocence and commitment by sending an angel to keep the lions from eating him. The king then ordered all those who had brought charges against Daniel to be thrown into the same pit with their wives and children. They were ripped to pieces before they reached the bottom of the pit. The king then commanded everyone in his kingdom to worship and honor the God of Daniel who honors the commitment of His people and sets them free by the working of great miracles.

Our next case study is taken from the third book of Daniel. This time our focus is on the three young Jewish men that were taken with Daniel; Shadrach, Meshach, and Abednego. These three young men were also appointed by the king to high positions in the Babylonian province and like Daniel they were also targets of Babylonian officials.

King Nebuchadnezzar built a ninety-foot statue in a valley near the city of Babylon. He commanded that as soon as the musical instruments started to play, everyone must bow down and worship the statue that the King had built or be immediately thrown into a flaming furnace. The Babylonian officials used this as an opportunity to find fault with the three Hebrew boys knowing they were committed to worshiping their God only. After hearing that the three Jewish boys refused to worship the statue, King Nebuchadnezzar was furious and sent for the three young men.

He offered to give them another chance but they refused to worship any God but their own. In anger, the king ordered the furnace to be heated seven times hotter than usual and commanded his strongest soldiers to tie them up and throw them into the furnace. Their outcome was the same as Daniel's. Their God delivered them out of the fire with no burns and no evidence that they had ever been in a fire. King Nebuchadnezzar praised their

God for sending an angel to rescue them and praised them for choosing to die rather than turn back on their commitment to worship or serve any god except their own.

Our final case study on commitment takes us to the Book of Acts, Chapter 5. Here in Jerusalem after Pentecost we see the apostles continuing the miraculous work of Jesus Christ; resulting in great multitudes of men and women being added to the Lord. This angered the high priest and the Sadducees who had the apostles arrested and thrown into the common prison. The next day when the high priest and the council sent to have the prisoners brought in, they found the prison doors shut and the guards in place but the apostles were gone.

V.19-20 *"But the angel of the Lord by night opened the prison doors, and brought them forth, and said ^{20}Go, stand and speak in the temple to the people all the words of this life".*

After being notified that the apostles were back at the temple teaching the people, officers were dispatched to bring them to the council. When the apostles were asked by the high priest why they disobeyed his orders not to teach in the name of Jesus, the apostles answered, "We ought to obey God rather than men". Again we see commitment to God, even when self-preservation is at stake. After this the high priest and the council had the apostles beaten and commanded them not to speak in the name of Jesus and let them go. But verses 41-42 tells us *"And they departed from the presence of the council, rejoicing that they were counted worthy to suffer shame for his name. ^{42}And daily in the temple, and in every house, they ceased not to teach and preach Jesus Christ".* Remember, a true commitment to God is rooted in the decision not to turn back regardless of the situation or the consequences.

In the three examples we used for our case study on commitment we can draw four key conclusions:

1) A commitment to the purposes of God guarantees or obligates God to move on His behalf by moving on yours.
2) A commitment takes the responsibility of accomplishing purpose off of you and puts it on God.
3) A commitment puts you on the prepared path that leads to

the good works and the good life that God pre-ordained for you.

4) Our commitment to God will cause us to be a visible, viable conduit in the earth realm for the power of God to flow through. It will produce signs and wonders for the entire world to see. This forces the world to acknowledge a power source that is beyond man's ability.

Three Characteristics of the Committed Believer

#1: The commitment outweighs the consequences

There will be times when backing out of your commitment will be tempting for the sake of a way that seems easier or better. The problem with this is, every time something comes along that seems easier or better you will be tempted again and again. More than likely you'll end up being tossed to and fro, following the doctrine of men and the lust of your flesh. We must learn not to be moved by the joy of comfort or the fear of consequences but remain focused on the commitment that produces the promises of God

#2: Focuses on Gods desired outcome and not intermediate observations and situations.

God has a desired outcome for every situation you will ever face in your life and this should always be the result that you seek. Where you end up is determined by how you handle where you are now and your commitment to stay the course. The tried, tested and true way to keep you from being moved off course by current observations and adverse situations is to remain focused and committed to God's desired outcome. We can always find encouragement in this area by *"Looking unto Jesus the author and finisher of our faith; who for the joy that was set before him endured the cross, despising the shame, and is set down at the right hand of the throne of God"* (Hebrews 12:2). Commitment gives us the ability to go through what we have to go through to get where God wants us to be.

#3: Counts the cost

In Luke 14:26-33 Jesus reinforces the concept of counting the cost. He makes it clear that before you commit to certain undertakings you should first count the cost to make sure you have the resources and the willingness to produce the desired result. Using that same concept I want to ask you a question. Have you counted the cost of not being committed? Have you ever taken the time to sit down and count the cost of missing destiny, not fulfilling purpose and never experiencing true personal fulfillment? Have you counted the cost of never doing what you were born to do? Psalm 37:5 tells us when we commit to God and trust in Him, He will bring His purpose for our lives to pass. I dare say it's time to count the cost.

Five Focus Points for the Believer Committed to Destiny Pursuit

In order to reach destiny and fulfill purpose you will most likely not be able to stay where you are and continue to do what you're doing. There will need to be changes in your attitude, actions and possibly your environment. There has to be a pulling up and away from the things that are holding you where you are, along with an ongoing commitment not to go back. This has to be intentional and systematic with a constant focus on things that will keep you moving forward. Let's look at what I consider to be five key focus points for a believer committed to destiny fulfillment.

1) Commitment to not going back.

There must be a commitment to not willingly go back and continue to do what you have been delivered or rescued from. 2 Peter 2:20-22 (CEV) says this, *When they learned about our Lord and Savior Jesus Christ, they escaped from the filthy things of this world. But they are again caught up and controlled by these filthy things, and now they are in worse shape than they were at first. 21They would have been better off if they had never known about the right way. Even after they knew what was right, they turned their backs on the holy commandments that they were given. 22What happened to them is just like the true saying, A dog will come back to lick up its own vomit. A pig that has been washed will roll in the mud*." This scripture makes it very clear that once we experience the overcoming and freeing power of God working in us, through us and on our behalf, then willingly go back to the mess that He got us out of, it will most assuredly be worse than it was before. I remember coming to the realization that if I leaned on God and not myself I could and would stay clean. I would literally feel His power overcoming and overriding my weaknesses, enabling me to resist what I could not resist on my own. I knew if I didn't let Him go, He wouldn't let me go. My flesh and my mind, however, kept telling me "It won't be as bad if I go back. I'm stronger now than I was before, I won't get hooked again. This time I will be able to keep it under control". I can tell you from experience that God's Word is true, it was not better, I was not stronger and I still did not have control. Every time I went back I started right where I left off and slid down fast from there. In various fellowships, this is called a relapse which means to fall back, slip or lose your footing. Today, let's just call it what the Word calls it, "a dog mentality" which convinces a human being that going back and re-eating what made you sick before won't make you sicker this time. Obviously this is a cycle of self-destructive behavior that must be stopped in order to forge ahead.

My favorite story about being committed to not going back happened over twenty years ago when a friend I was sponsoring in Narcotics Anonymous called me from a rehab center. He had about five years clean from drugs and alcohol. Naturally my first question was "Are you alright?" and with a happy voice he replied he was fine. By now I'm kind of confused and thinking - you're in rehab which means you had to relapse so why do you sound happy and how could you be fine? I asked him "What did you do?" He answered "Nothing". Now, I'm no longer kind of confused - I'm really confused. I asked "Why are you in rehab if you didn't do anything?" He told me the temptation to use had become so strong he didn't think he could resist it on his own, so he checked himself into a ten day program. He was not willing to take a chance on going back into that life because he had made a commitment to God and to himself not to use. He was willing to do whatever he had to, to keep that commitment. For believers it's alright if you need to check yourself back in, but it works better if we never check ourselves out. We must always remember that it is not our power, but the prevailing power of God that keeps us from falling and if we never let Him go; He will never let us down. Don't get me wrong, grabbing hold to God when you fall is a good thing, but never letting go is better because it will keep you from falling.

The second point I want to make as it relates to not going back is, every good and perfect gift comes from God and God deserves and demands His credit. The world's way of maintaining an attitude of success is to take the credit for what you have accomplished and what you have acquired. As believers we must be very careful to guard against this mindset, for scripture tells us we can do nothing without God. With this in mind, take a minute to read Deuteronomy 8:10-19. This scripture reminds us not to forget the blessings of God and take personal credit for what He has done in our lives.

The word 'perish' in verse nineteen is a Hebrew word that means "to wander away, lose oneself, vanish, go astray or be destroyed". Simply put, this is when you relinquish the blessings that God has released into your life by causing the same God that moved for you, to move against you. We must always remember that pride, self-conceit and self-confidence has the potential to lead us away from God and cause us to lean on ourselves rather than God. The scripture is very clear in reminding us that God is our deliverer, provider, protector and the one that gives us the power to get wealth. God, though He is a loving God, is also a jealous God who will not stand for us to take credit or give credit to someone else for what He alone has done. Anytime you take your focus off God you have to put it somewhere else. This act of shifting your focus will also shift your direction and lead you away from God, His power and His purpose.

The last point I want to make on this before we move on, is that you must always keep your momentum going forward aimed at the new. In Philippians 3:13-14 Paul says *"Brethren, I count not myself to have apprehended: but this one thing I do, forgetting those things which are behind, and reaching forth unto those things which are before, [14] I press toward the mark for the prize of the high calling of God in Christ Jesus"*. This scripture has many important points but we will only focus on three. First: we need to have a one-track mind or be single-minded in our focus to move forward in the things of God. Second: we can't rest on our past success nor should we stress on our past mistakes. Paul says he's forgetting the things that are behind. We don't need to remember, reminisce, return to view or try to go back and retrieve what we have put behind us. When we are focusing on where we've been, we are not focused on where we're going. It's like driving your car while looking through the rear view mirror. You will either turn the car toward what you are looking at or hit something that could have and should have been avoided. Your past is not a testament of where God can take you; it's a testimony of what he has already taken you through.

Third: we must reach. This means we become willing to step outside of our current level of comfort and stretch ourselves towards that which surpasses our current expectations. We force ourselves to grow by disciplining ourselves to diligently do the things we were unable or unwilling to do before. Once you began to reach, you realize that where you are now is not the issue because you don't have to stay there much longer. You will understand it is where you're going that counts and your current location will become your next testimony; and triumph. With this in mind you make a commitment to make every word you say and every step you take, a momentum producing paddle stroke that forces you closer and closer to the purposes of God for you.

2) Commitment to destiny pursuit

Once you decide you're not going back, you must now decide where you're going to. Make destiny fulfillment your desired destination. Understand that reaching destiny is not like driving to Chicago and then saying you're there. It's more like a preordained set of events and circumstances on the road to Chicago that prepare, propel and make provision for you to perform God's will upon arrival. Pursuing destiny is not a fixed location or a one-time event; it's a lifestyle that always seeks God's desired outcome at every rest stop, mile marker and landmark along the way. Pursuing destiny is not planning for tomorrow; it's performing God's will today. Ephesians 2:10 reminds us that our purpose was planned beforehand. The paths that lead to the purpose were prepared ahead of time and the good life God wants us to experience has already been prearranged and made ready. In other words, you don't make destiny - you find it. Based on this scripture there are three points I want you to internalize.

#1: Since your purpose was planned ahead of time, God decided who He needed you to be before He created you. Then He created you to be just what He needed you to be. Accordingly, everything you need to accomplish your purpose and reach your destiny was front-loaded in you when God recreated you.

#2: Since the paths that lead to that purpose have already been prepared, everything you need has already been placed on the paths. Somewhere between where you are now and where God needs you to be is what you need to get exposed to, the people you need to get connected with and the developmental opportunities you need to go through. These paths are also like GPS indicators in that they let you know where you are and give you a sense of where you're headed. If you look back over the last few years of your life and study the path you were on, it will surely help you to understand why you are where you are now; good, bad, or indifferent.

#3: To understand the prearranged good life in the context of Ephesians 2:10, you need to realize that at the same time God was planning the good works, preparing the paths and prearranging the good life - He was also planning you. This is critical because the good life is predicated on everything that is in you, everything that you will go through and everything that God has called you to do. The good life that God has prepared is the only life that will produce lasting satisfaction and complete fulfillment. God the Creator, is the only one who knows what will make your life fulfilled. Let's be honest, if we knew what would fulfill us, we probably would not have done half of the dumb things we did in search of fulfillment. The good life is not something that we can earn, manufacture or buy because it is God's reward for those who do the good works, stay on the paths, pursue destiny and fulfill purpose.

3) Commitment to study the Word of God

2Timothy 2:15 says we should "*Study to shew thyself approved unto God, a workman that needeth not to be ashamed, rightly dividing the word of truth*". The word 'study' used here is the

Greek word "spoudazo" and it is not the word you usually think of when you think of a student. This word is indicative of "a workman or one who diligently endeavors, or exerts himself to be approved by God". This workman will be tested, tried and approved by the one issuing or allowing the test. This workman understands that the results of the test are not predicated on the challenge, but on his ability to correctly apply biblical principles in that challenge. For a believer the challenge is never the issue, it is always the response that determines the outcome. Biblical principles correctly applied in faith will always produce biblical promises and the only way you can correctly interpret and apply the Word of God is through study. The Word of God is the tool that works in every situation, but every good carpenter will tell you the tool is only as good as your ability to use it correctly.

The Bible is the instruction manual on Godly living which is why 2Timothy 3:16-17 tells us that *"All scripture is given by inspiration of God, and is profitable for doctrine, for reproof, for correction, for instruction in righteousness: [17]That the man of God may be perfect, thoroughly furnished unto all good works"*. Four seemingly simple words used in this scripture clearly communicate the importance of making the regular, systematic study of God's Word a must for every believer. The words are doctrine, reproof, correction and instruction. Doctrine gives us the established order of God, or God's view and perspectives on life. Reproof is the admonishing, convicting, exposing and dismantling of our erroneous or wrong thinking. Correction is to straighten up or restore by the assimilation of God's truth into our thinking and decision making process. This means we replace our imperfect and inconsistent thinking with the perfect word and will of God. Instruction is to teach God's systematic way to live, having the spirit of God as your tutor and the Word of God as the primary source for educating yourself to live the life God desires.

The Word of God is what equips, empowers and enables the believer to be thoroughly furnished in having everything needed and required by God to stay on the path, do the good works and live the good life. In essence, this scripture tells us that the wisdom we need from God about how God functions, thinks and wants us to think and function is all laid out for us in a systematic, step by step instruction book we call the Bible. Joshua 1:8 (ESV) says

"This Book of the Law shall not depart from your mouth, but you shall meditate on it day and night, so that you may be careful to do according to all that is written in it. For then you will make your way prosperous, and then you will have good Success". Again this tells us that our success is not influenced by our situations, but by our ability to apply God's Word in them. Therefore, the Bible is the road map to successful Christian living and any believer who does not study the map will be unsuccessful, defenseless against the attacks of the enemy, unable to access the promises of God and in a permanent state of self-imposed bondage.

4) Committed to a lifestyle of prayer

The word 'prayer' is probably one of the most mentioned, yet under-applied words used by believers today. We say, "I'll pray for this", or "I'll pray for that", but do we really understand the importance and the power of prayer. Luke 18:1 says *"And he spake a parable unto them to this end, that men ought always to pray, and not to faint"*. 1Thessalonians 5:17 instructs us to *"Pray without ceasing"*. This tells us that at all times, under all conditions - no matter the circumstances, good or bad - prayer must be a priority. Easton's 1897 Bible dictionary defines prayer: "to converse with God; the intercourse of the soul with God not in contemplation or meditation but in direct address to him, a beseeching the Lord and the pouring out of ones soul before the Lord".

Prayer is also a way for believers, God's children, to show our faith and trust in Him by praying to a God we cannot see, while believing He hears us and that he's able and willing to answer our prayers. Our contextual definitions of prayer are, "1) the predetermined process/path of communicating with God. 2) The channel of access established by God whereby His children tap into His power, perception and loving kindness so that all needs; provisional, directional and relational may be met". In essence, prayer is communion with God where we open ourselves to him, thus opening a path for Him to share Himself with us. Prayer is the turning of the soul to God. In Psalms 25:1 David describes prayer as the lifting up of the living soul to the living God when he says, *"unto Thee, O Lord, do I lift up my soul."*

As believers, our walk with Christ is based on the depth of our relationship with Him, and the depth of our relationship is based on the level of our commitment and communion with Him. Therefore, we can know God and not be close, we can be near God and not feel His presence, and we can speak out to Him, but never hear His voice. In other words, a lack of commitment, communion and communication will bring about a lack of spiritual development and intimacy in our relationship with God our Father. To the question, how do we communicate with God? The answer is prayer. My intent here is not to teach you how to pray, but to emphasize the importance of a commitment to being instant in prayer. I believe prayer is the greatest power on earth, for the Bible tells us that prayer moves the Hand that moves the world. To make sure this point is sealed in your minds, let's take a brief look at three key benefits of a life commitment to prayer.

#1: Prayer keeps you from being consumed by the cares of this life. Luke 21:34-36 says *"And take heed to yourselves, lest at any time your hearts be overcharged with surfeiting, and drunkenness, and cares of this life, and so that day come upon you unawares. [35] For as a snare shall it come on all them that dwell on the face of the whole earth. [36]Watch ye therefore, and pray always, that ye may be accounted worthy to escape all these things that shall come to pass, and to stand before the Son of man."* In the purest context, this scripture is talking about Christ's prophecy of the destruction of Jerusalem, and tells us how to prepare for His second coming. I also believe it is telling us the only way we will be able to properly handle everything that's going to happen, and is already happening in these last days, is to watch and pray. Through watching and prayer we can handle life's ups and downs without being overcome by fear, stress and stupidity and avoid returning to a lifestyle that brought us only momentary comfort in the past. Watching will keep us aware of the things that can be seen. Prayer will keep us aware of the things that can't be seen and give us God's direction on how to handle them both.

#2: To follow the example of Christ benefits believers. We read in 1 John 2:6 *"He that saith he abideth in him ought himself also so to walk, even as he walked"*. If we are one with Christ, or profess to be united to Him, then we ought to imitate Him in all things. His life should be the example and the blueprint we follow to achieve godly living. Matthew 26:36 tells us that in the Garden of Gethsemane Jesus prepared Himself through prayer for what would prove to be the hardest day of His life. Mark 1:35 says *"And in the morning, rising up a great while before day, he went out, and departed into a solitary place, and there prayed"*. Here we see the Savior, who was perfectly holy, regard communion with God through prayer of great importance. This also shows (as in Matthew 26) a pattern of prayer before making prevalent decisions. Prayer was not only important to Jesus when He was here on earth, Romans 8:34 tells us that right now, right at this very moment as you are reading this chapter, Jesus is sitting on the right hand of the Father praying for you and for me.

#3: Prayer is the channel of access to receive what you need from God. 2 Peter 1:3 tells us that *"According as his divine power hath given unto us all things that pertain unto life and godliness, through the knowledge of him that hath called us to glory and virtue:"* This means we have been given everything we need to live the life that God has called us to live and to live it in a way that is holy and acceptable to God. So if God has given us, or made available to us, everything we need to live the life He created us to live, what is the problem or what are we missing? Before I answer that question let's take a quick look at what I call the principles of availability and accessibility. Let's use the promises as an example. The promises tell us what's available, they tell us what God wants us to have and what He has made available for us to have. Even though the promises tell us what's available, Hebrews 6:12 tells us they are only accessible through faith and patience. So faith and patience are the principles that need to be applied to take actual possession of what's available. This means we can know what we can have, but if we're not willing to do what God requires, we will never take possession of what technically already belongs to us. This is because the same one who makes the promises available, is the same one who gets to decide the predetermined process to access the promise. God says we have not because we ask not which identifies prayer as a key component in gaining access and taking possession of the promises that have been made available to all believers. Remember, prayer is the channel of access established by God whereby His children tap into His power, providence, perception and loving kindness so that all needs; provisional, directional and relational may be met.

5) A commitment to live by faith.

Hebrew 10:38 tells us that the just shall live by faith. This simply means that the just person or the person in right standing with God will live by faith. I think it's interesting that the Bible says we are to live by faith and not in faith. The word 'by' means "from, out of, because of or by reason of". Therefore to live by faith is to live in a constant confidence in the power of something outside of self. This allows our faith to supersede past mistakes and current conditions because our faith is not in us, but comes out of our knowledge of someone greater than us. He is someone who supersedes circumstances, has unlimited power and a commitment to using it on our behalf. The word "live" is the Greek word "Zao" which means "to breathe, be among the living, to enjoy real life, to be fresh, strong, efficient, and powerful, to have true life and be endless in the kingdom of God".

The true Christian experience can only be experienced through a life lived by faith. Faith is so critical to successful Christian living. I believe every believer should have their own personal prayer meditations that they rehearse periodically. Here are a few of my faith meditations you can use as an example: Faith in God, is the ground under my feet that keeps me from falling or failing, without it I would lose hope and crumble under the constant pressures of life. Faith in God is the invisible force that produces visible outcomes and turns obstacles into opportunities and opportunities into testimonies. Without it I would see my situations as more than I can handle, instead of the handle that opens the door to my next testimony. Faith in God is the fuel that gives me the energy to finish the race under difficult and extreme conditions, not just as a runner but as a winner. Without it I will be hesitant to take the next step that propels me to the next stop on my destiny path.

Biblically speaking if you are not living by faith, you are not really living. You just haven't physically died yet. I envision a life not lived by faith as being on a ventilator where you can hear life and you can see life but you just aren't able to fully participate. If you're not committed to live by faith, you will not be able to exercise your godly authority, envision your godly purpose or accept your godly inheritance.

We must always remember that our commitment to God will keep us tied to the purpose and the power that brings God's will for our lives to pass.

The Close

Truly we have covered a lot of ground in our discussion of empowerment and freedom through the seven key strategies in living a fulfilled life in Christ. Although freedom is a free gift from God, freedom itself will never produce God's desired outcome for your life. It will not bring you the fulfillment intended without trust in God, a change in your thinking and a commitment to scripture based living. What I have set out to do in this writing is to systematically walk you through a scripture based process, or set of principles, that will literally force true and lasting change in your life. It will cause you to use your freedom to serve God, serve others and pursue God's desired destiny for your life. I understand that just having a basic understanding of freedom is not enough. There has to be practical steps and principles you use your freedom to follow, that will lead you in a continual pursuit of God and His will for you. This process has to be so automatic it will be impossible to fail if you stay committed and refuse to quit. This means, the process has to be founded on biblical promises, yet triggered by biblical principles that unleash the power of God to cause His Word to come to pass in your life.

The process and principles I have just described were given to you in this writing; starting with the understanding that freedom gives you the authority and ability to choose to overcome any negative pattern or habit that you deem unproductive in your life. This understanding allows you to take ownership of your current dilemma, which means as the owner you have the right to choose what changes should and need to be made for your life to get back on track. Then, understanding the undeniable truth that God is in control, gives you the ability to replace your fears with faith and live a life that is pleasing to God and fulfilling for you. Faith in God allows you to walk with boldness and steadfastness through the vicissitudes of life due to an unwavering awareness that the unlimited power of God is providing protection, provision and purpose fulfillment in the midst of difficult times. When you know that God is in control and without limits you know that nothing can touch you unless God allows it and intends to use it for your good. Having this faith in God and the surety of His Word then forces you to understand that you have to be who His Word says you are because God cannot lie. This truth when internalized gives you the ability to conquer your flesh, the enemy and the world. It also makes you a threat and target of the enemy. At this point, learning to endure temptation becomes the next logical and critical key that keeps you from losing ground at the point of gaining life changing momentum. Once the enemy realizes he has no power over you, his only hope is to get you to misuse your freedom through acts of unforgiveness. Unforgiveness stops your momentum by placing you in a self-imposed prison that only forgiveness can get you out of. Mind renewal then becomes the ultimate tool for continuing the course of true and lasting change, because the mind is the place where all battles are fought and won by the believer. Lastly, commitment locks you into a daily application of the process and principles that will produce the purpose and desired outcome that God created and called you to fulfill.

Giving you these seven key biblical principles straight from the Word of God is my assignment as the author. Using the tools that will empower you to get free and stay free is your assignment as the reader. I pray that you will use the tools, change your life and allow God to do exceeding abundantly above all that you could ask or think, according to the power that works in you!

About the Author

William T. Bantom III is a deacon, principle teacher and men's ministry leader with a focus on breaking the patterns of the past. After spending much of his early life in bondage to drugs and alcohol, William has dedicated the last twenty-four years of his life to teaching others how to experience the promises of freedom contained in the Word of God.

William and his wife Loretta reside in Michigan where they have two children Ryan and Adrea along with four grandchildren.

Contact William via:

Email: empowered2befree@gmail.com
Web: www.williamtbantom.com
FB: Empowered to be Free
Twitter: @Empowered2BFree

References

Copyright Information

Amplified Bible:

New American Standard Bible

English Standard Version, ESV

Message

New Century Version

New King James Version
Scripture taken from the New King James Version®. Copyright © 1982 by Thomas Nelson. Used by permission. All rights reserved.

New Living Translation
Scripture quotations' marked (NLT) are taken from the Holy Bible, New Living Translation, copyright © 1996, 2004, 2007 by Tyndale House Foundation. Used by permission of Tyndale House Publishers, Inc., Carol Stream, Illinois 60188. All rights reserved.

Good News Bible
Scriptures marked as (GNB) are taken form the Good News Bible – Second Edition © 1992 By the American Bible Society.
Used by permission.

Contemporary English Version
Scriptures marked as "(CEV)" are taken from the Contemporary English Version © 1995 By American Bible Society.
Used by permission

King James Version
Scriptures marked as (KJV) are taken from the 1769 King James version also known as the Authorized Version.

e-sword – Strongs Exhaustive Concordance by James Strong, S.T.D LLC. published in 1890; public domain;

VISION

There is nothing that I will ever need that is more important than Jesus.

- Study the children of Israel's journey to freedom

- The very fact that their is evident the power of God is present. The enemy only attacks those who are a threat. Believers that know the truth. Is this a correct observation Lord?

- Looking
    - Alignment / re alignment
    - Realignment of truth
    - deliverance

CPSIA information can be obtained at www.ICGtesting.com
Printed in the USA
BVOW11s1850290415

398107BV00008B/12/P